SHARON BUYDENS

Best of Tiny House Photobook:
Color Pix - Cottage, Bungalow, Beach & Boathouse, Log Cabin, Mud Hut, Cave & Rock Dwelling, Yurt, & the Privy

SHARON BUYDENS

SHARON BUYDENS

Copyright © 2018 Sharon Buydens

All rights reserved.

ISBN: 1718656084
ISBN-13: 978-1718656086

SHARON BUYDENS

DEDICATION

For Tyler.

ABOUT THIS BOOK

This book is low-text with photographs, for your easy reading pleasure. Photos attributed to the Creative Commons and Pixabay, and many thanks to Raymond Orenda of Organic Food Kenya.

SHARON BUYDENS

SHARON BUYDENS

CONTENTS

Styles 2

Mountain Cottages 7

Farm Houses 9

Rock / Stone 10

Brick 11

Cave Houses 12

Beach Houses 13

Boathouses 18

Houseboats 20

Desert Dwellings & Mud Huts 21

Solar 23

Piers & Stilts 24

Towers 26

Log Cabins 28

Wood Homes 29

Bungalows 30

Thatch and Reeds 32

Yurts 34

Tipis & Wigwam 35

Whimsical 36

Other Stuff 37

Wheels 38

Privies 39

Domes 40

Sheds 41

Treehouses 42

SHARON BUYDENS

Styles

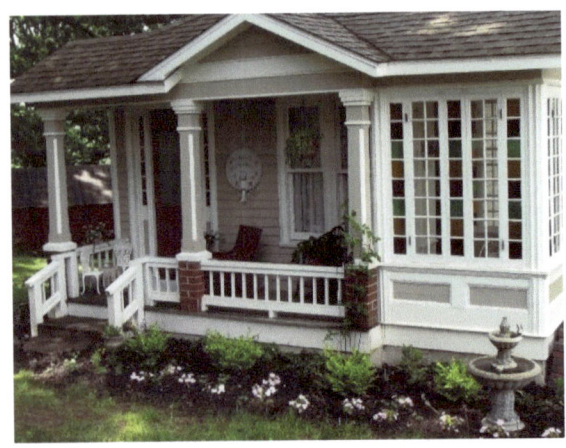

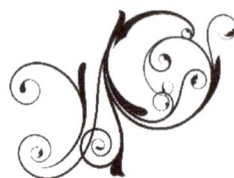

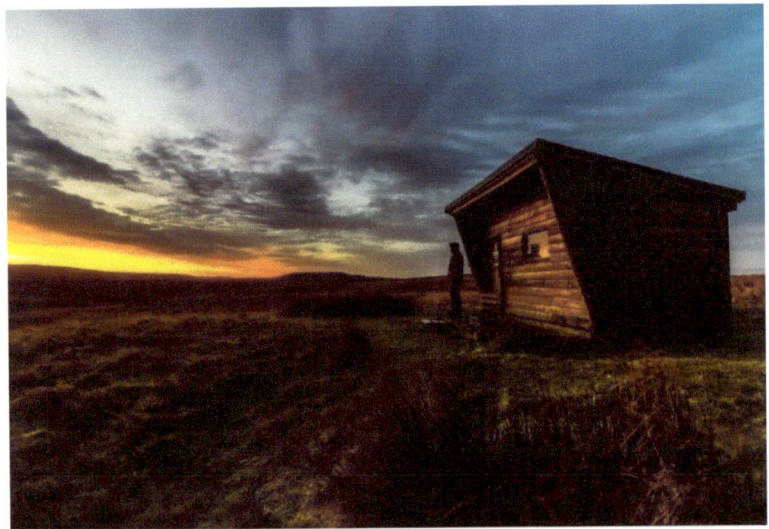

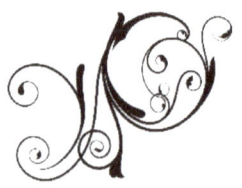

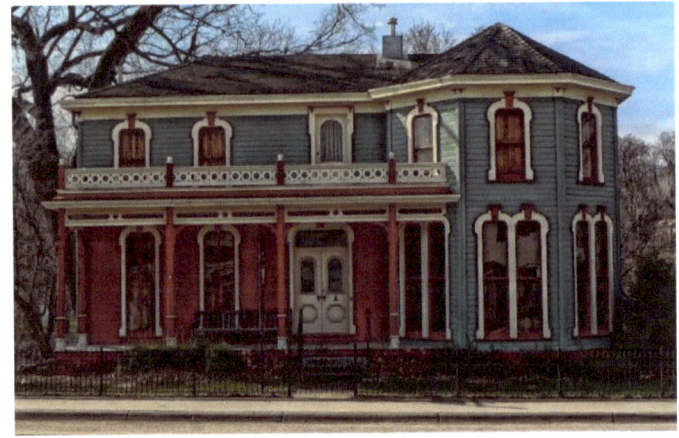

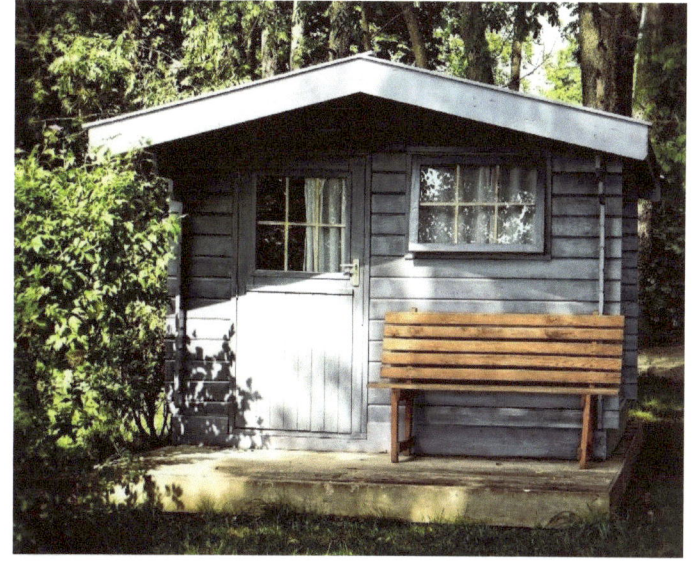
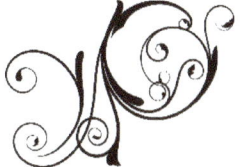
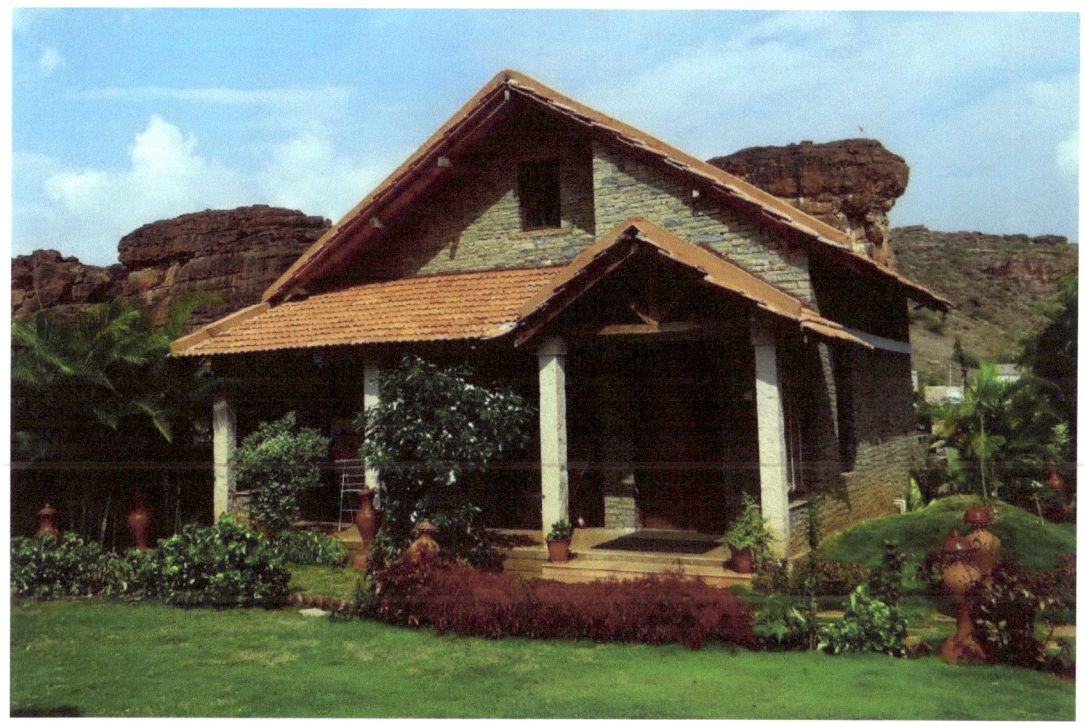
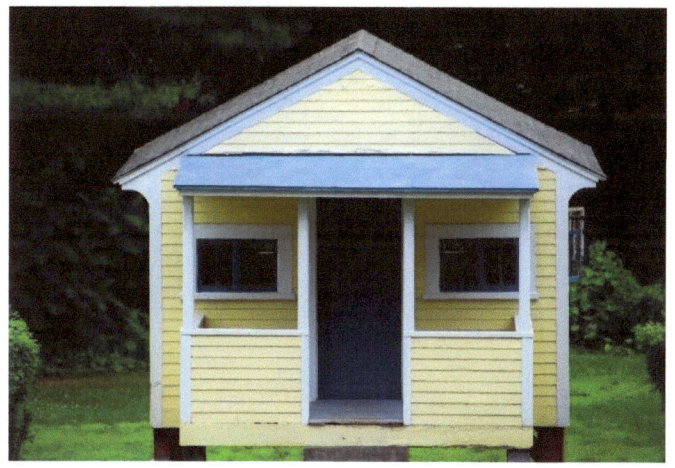
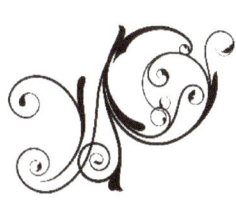

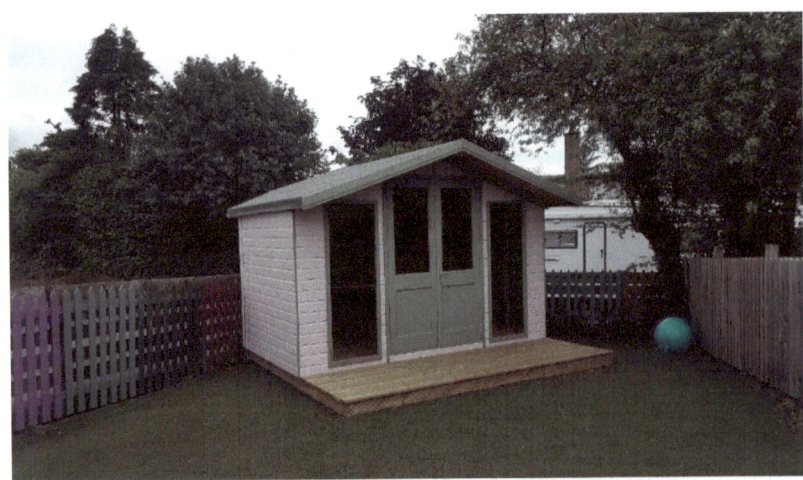
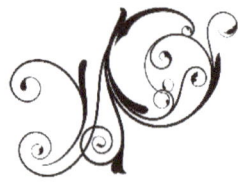
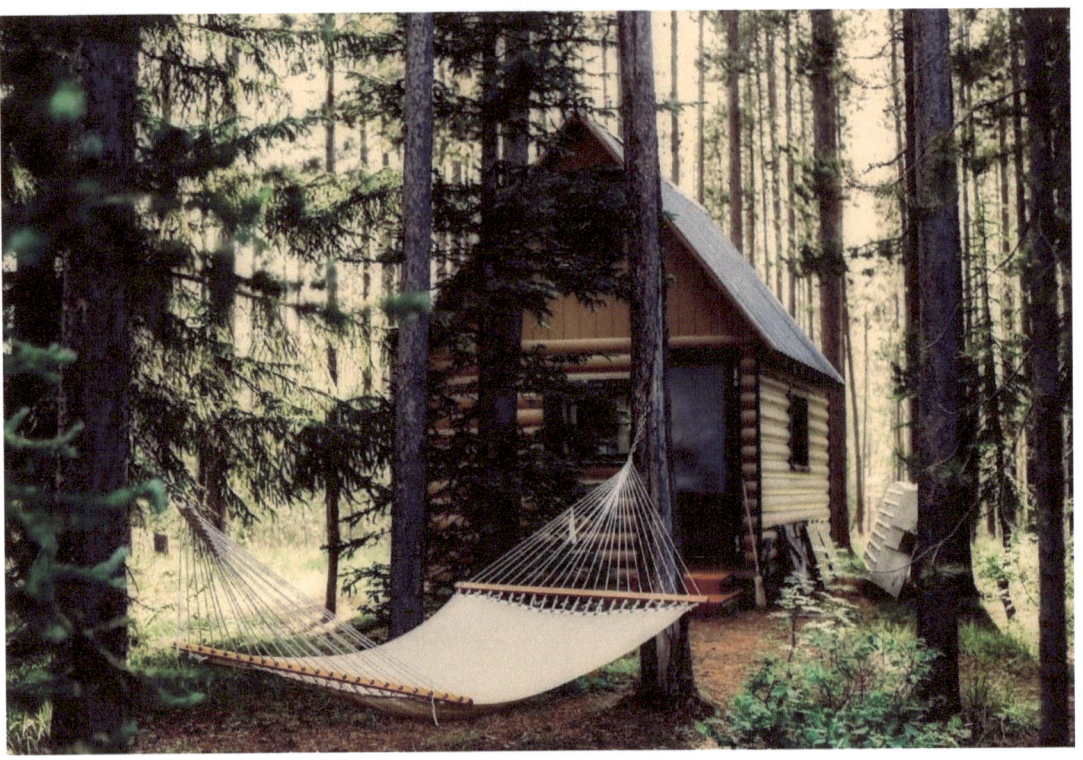
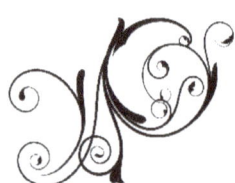
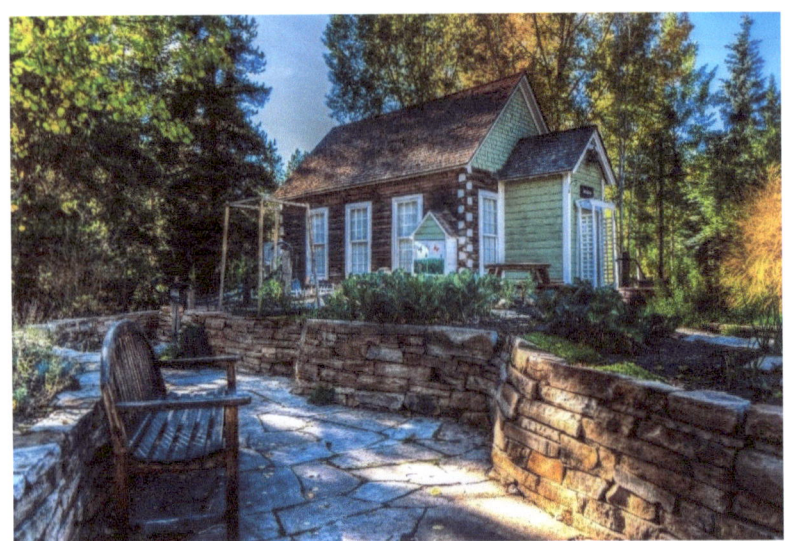

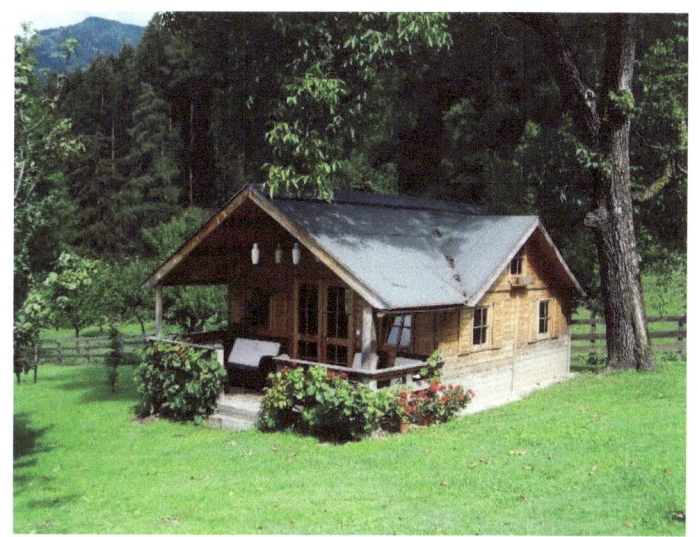

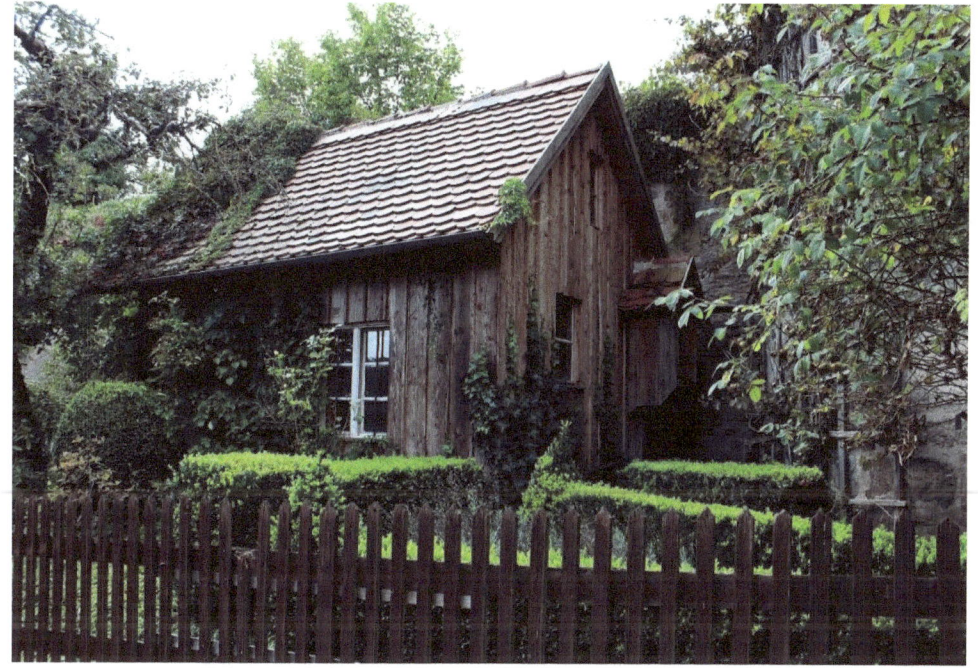

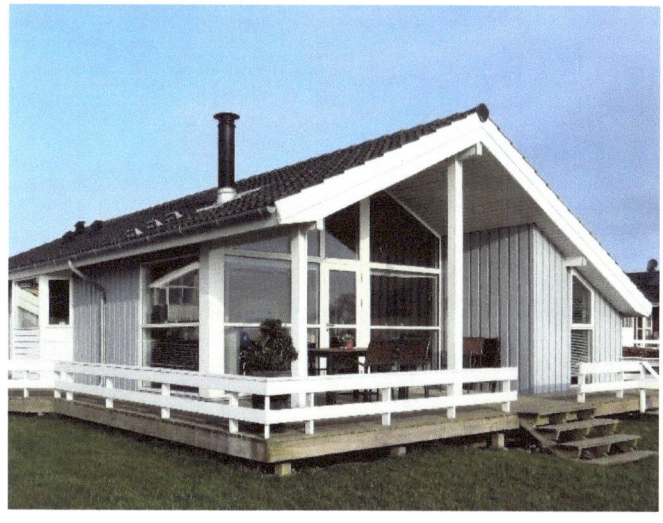

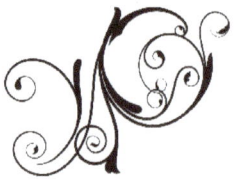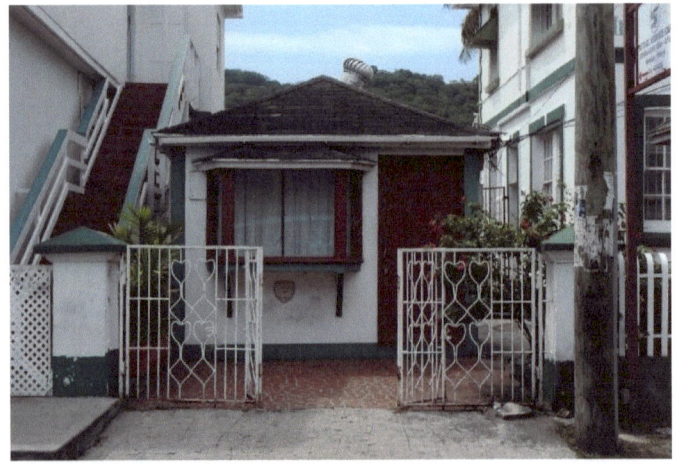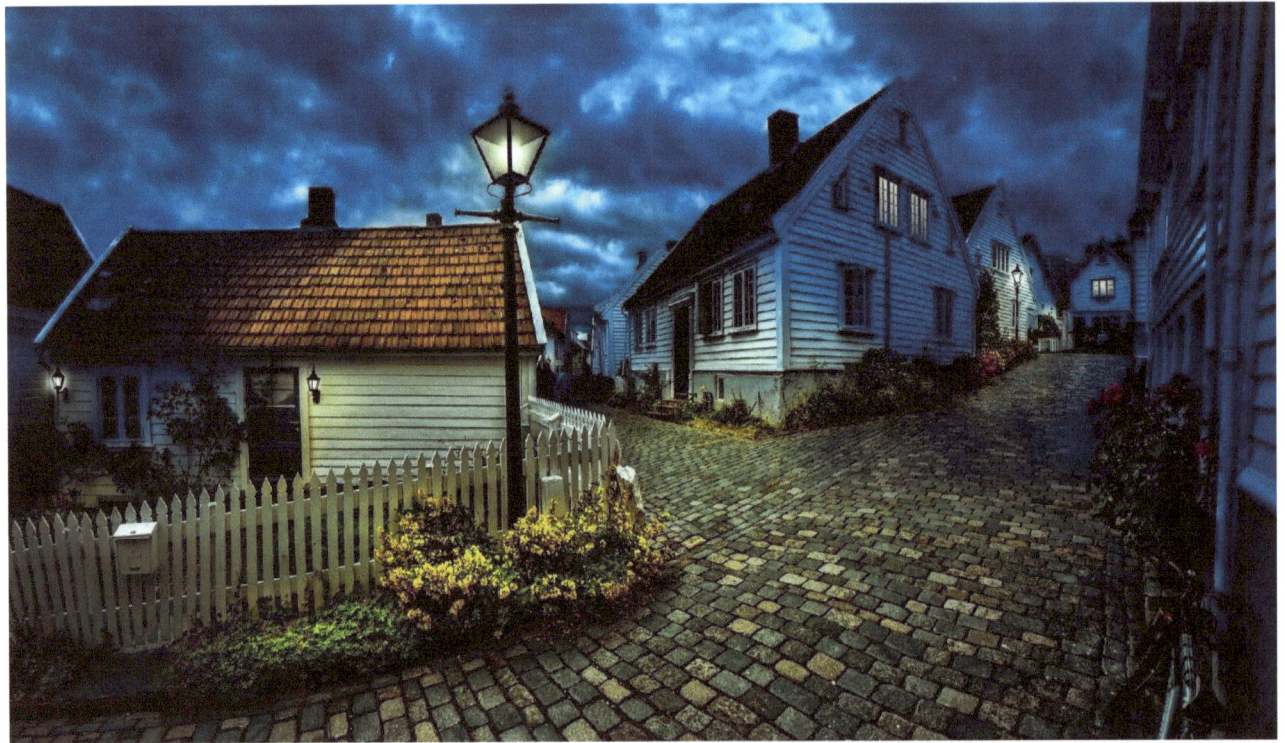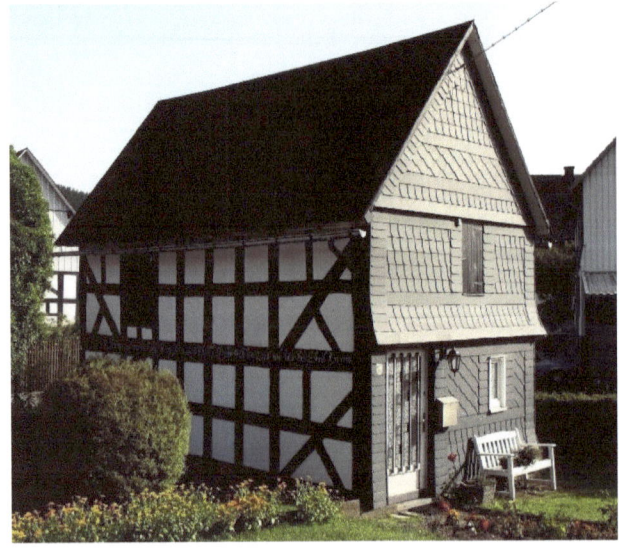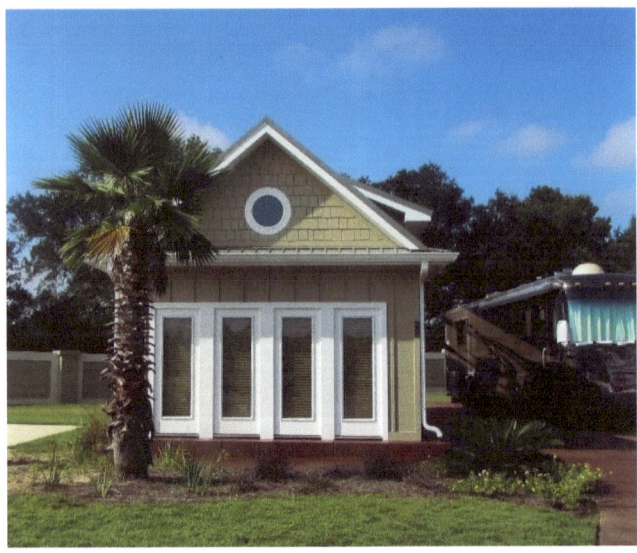

Mountain Cottages

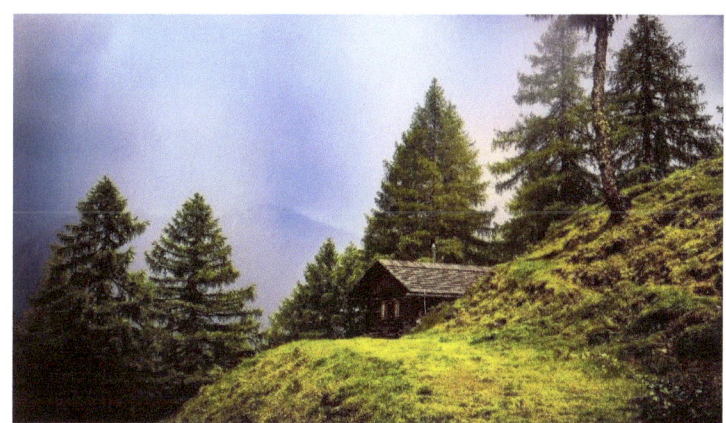

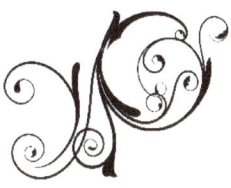

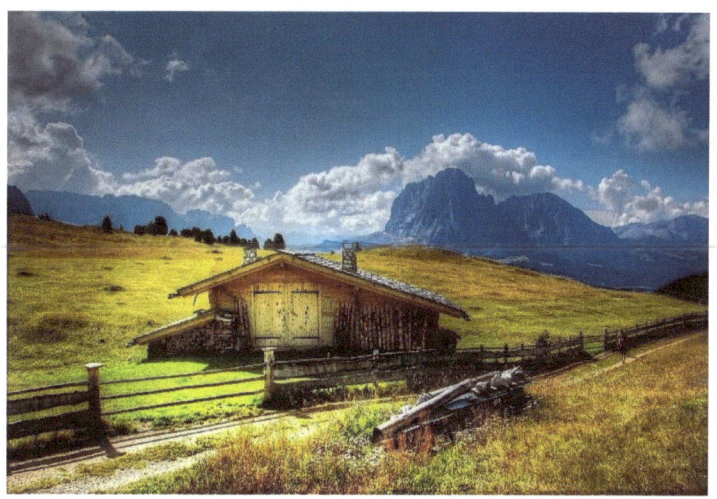

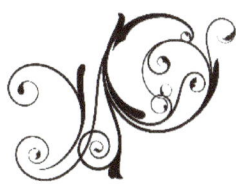

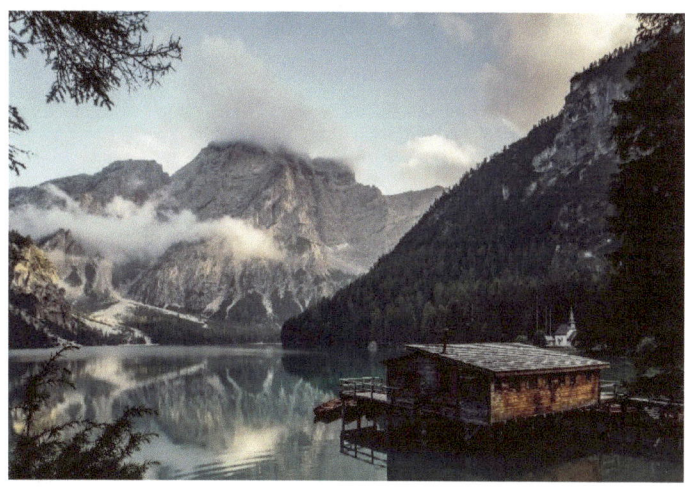

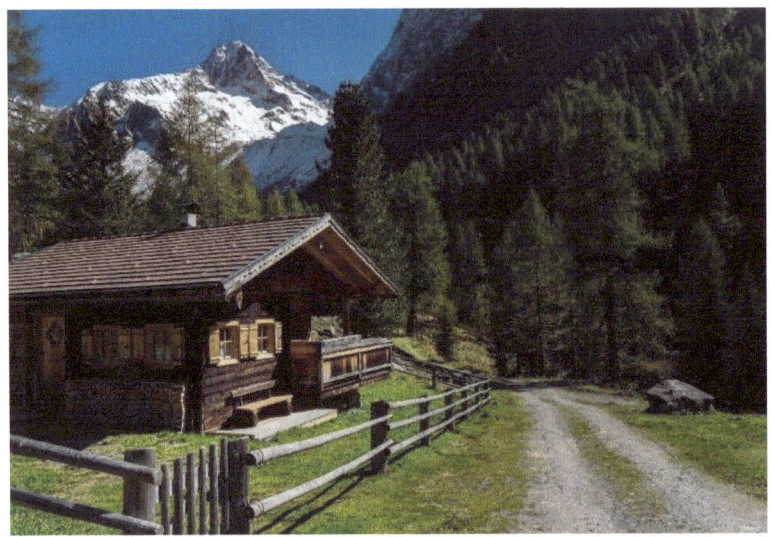
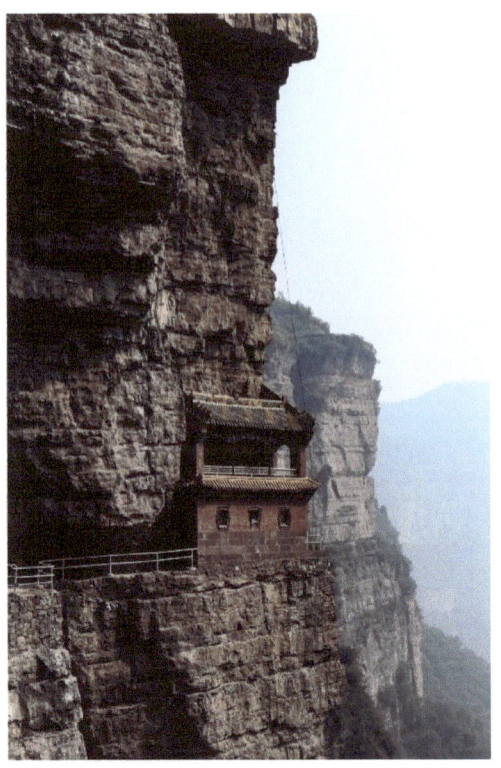
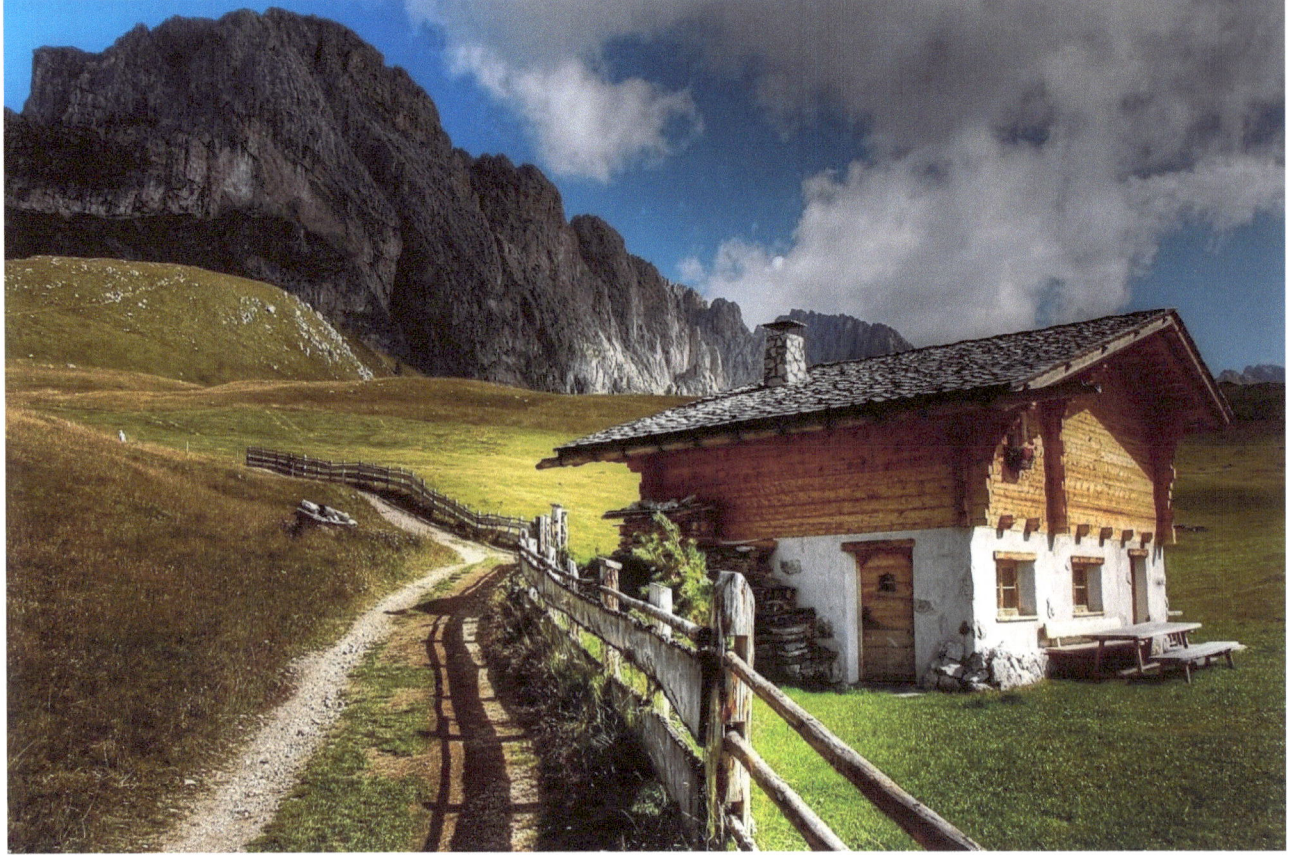

Farm Houses

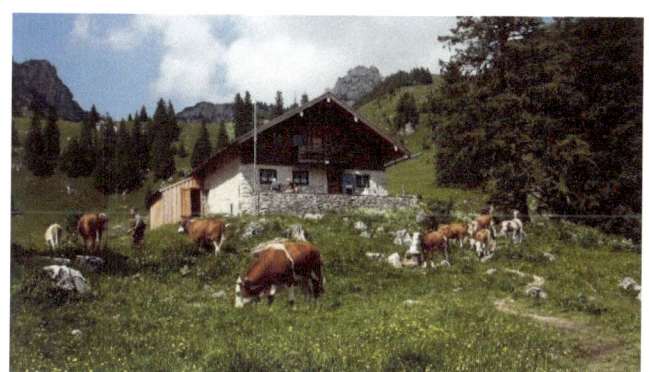
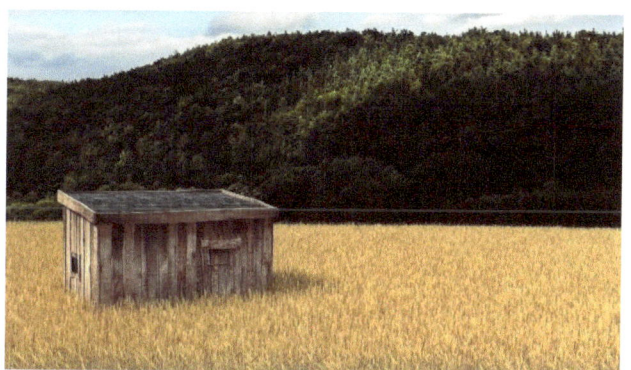
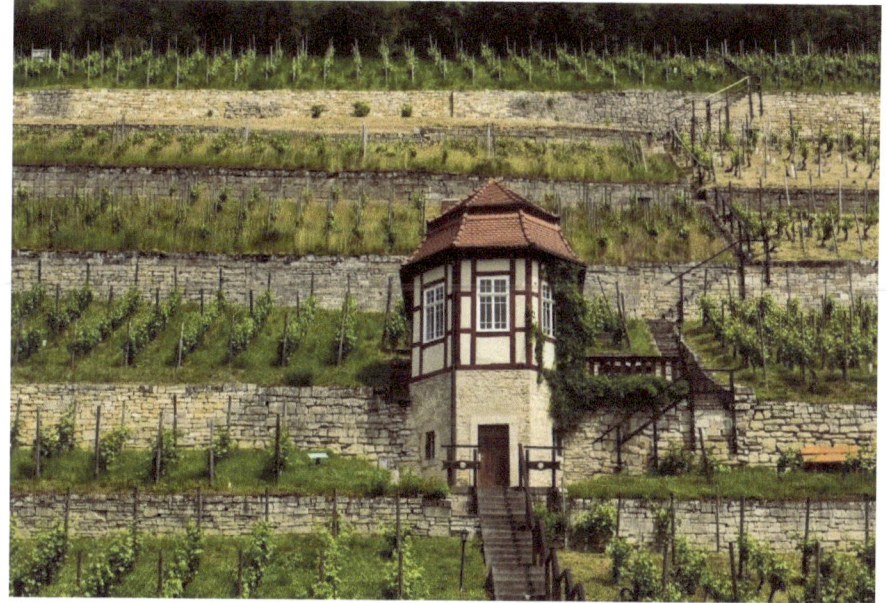
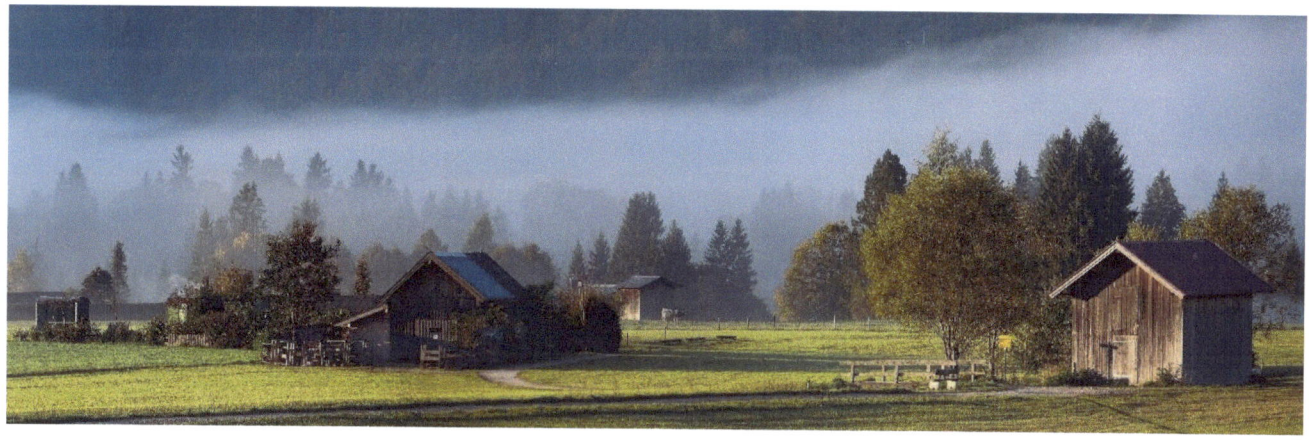

Rock / Stone

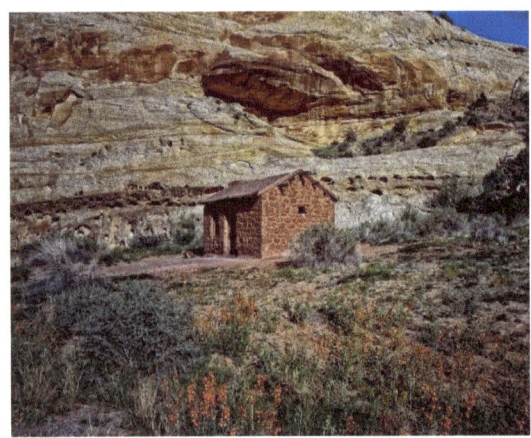
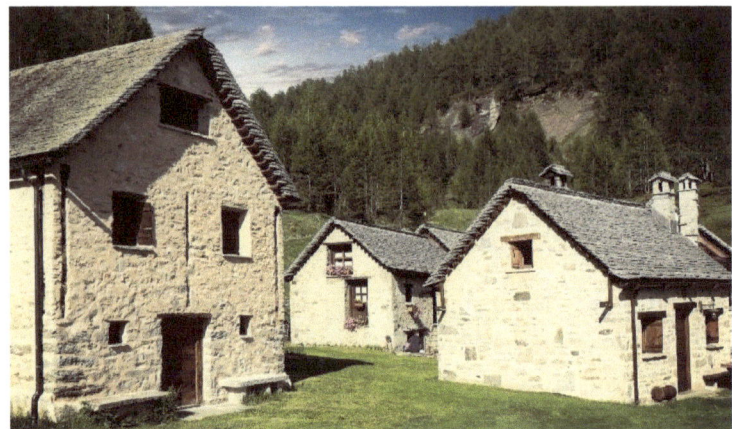
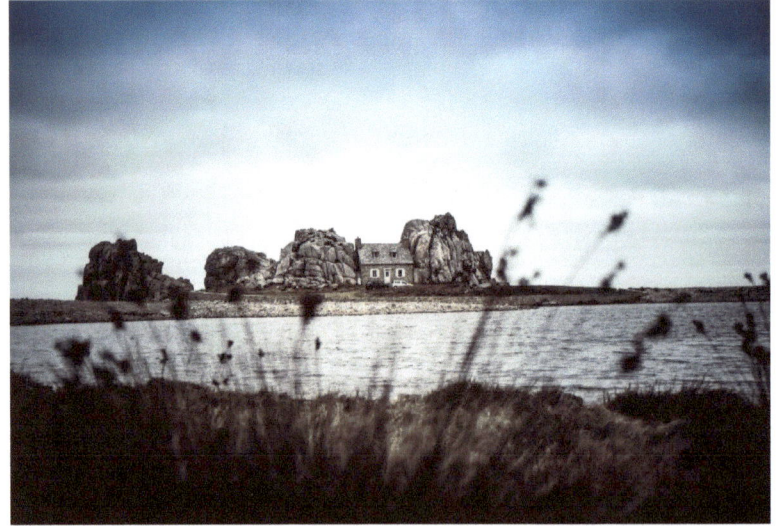
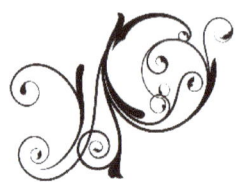
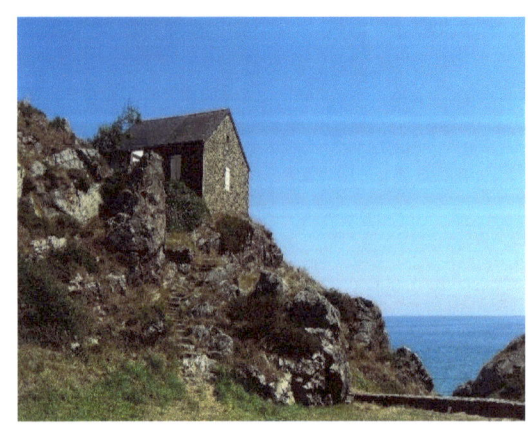

Brick

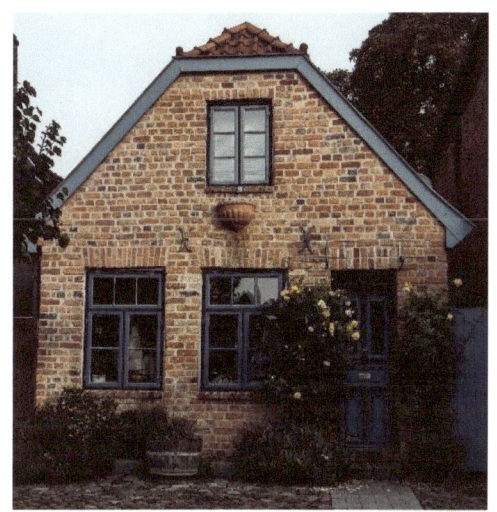
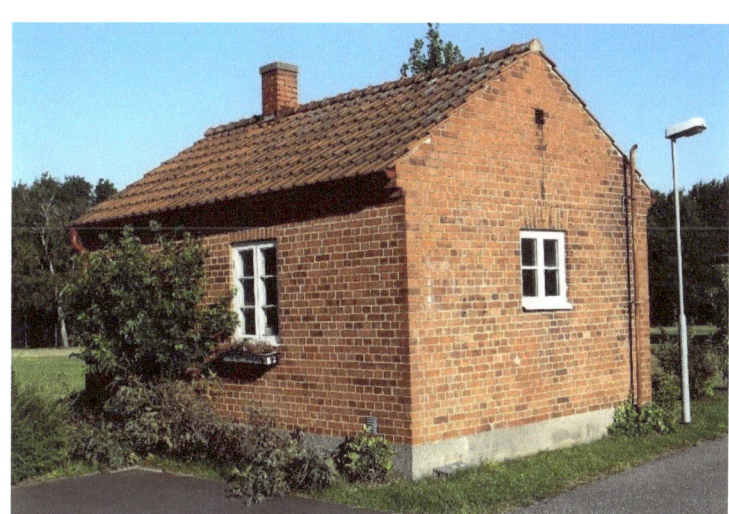
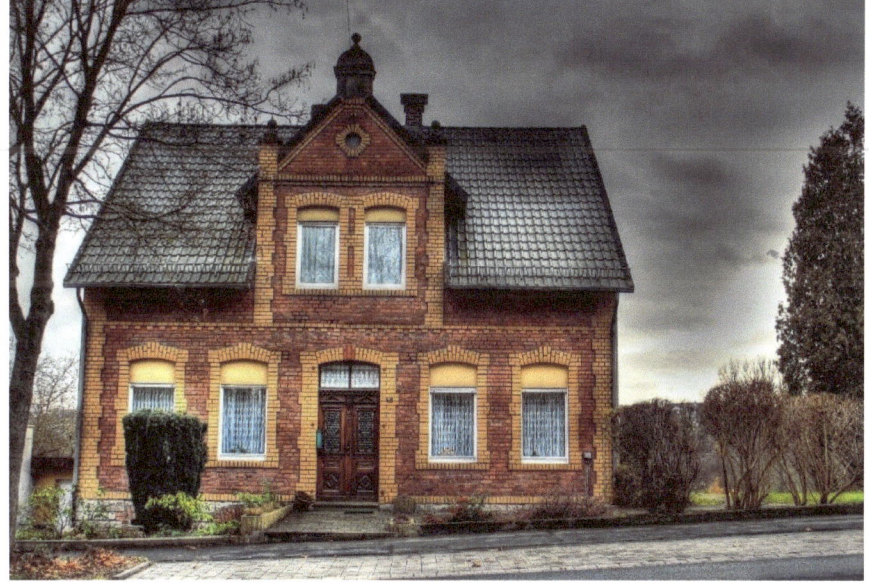
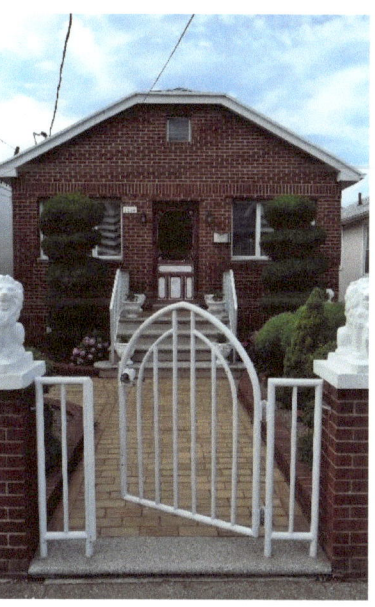
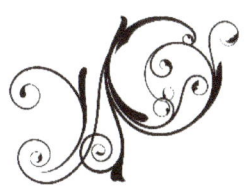

Cave Houses

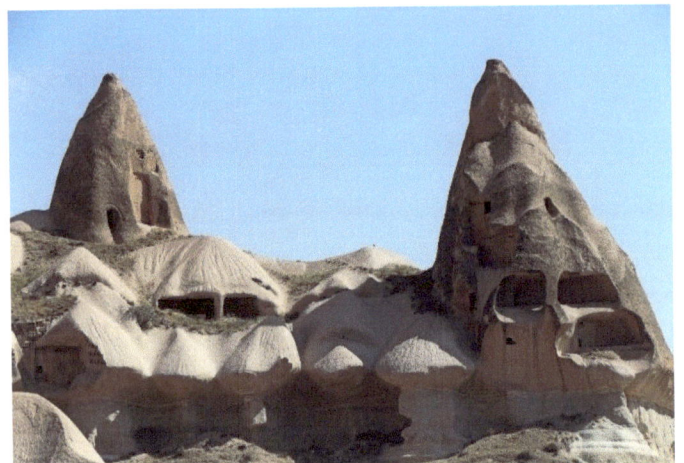

Cappadocia, Turkey

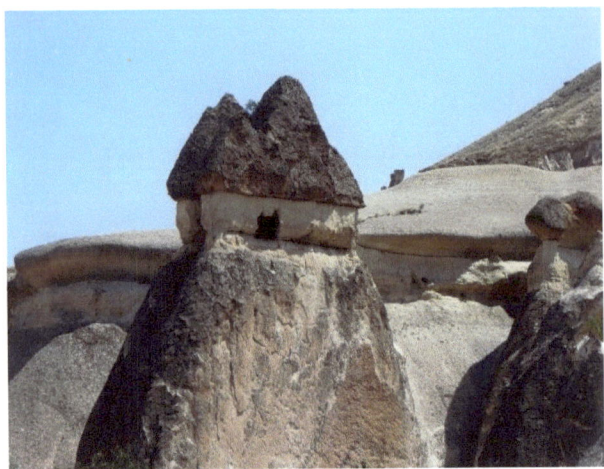

Cappadocia fairy chimneys

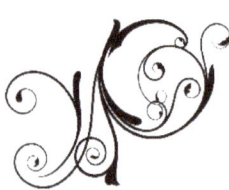

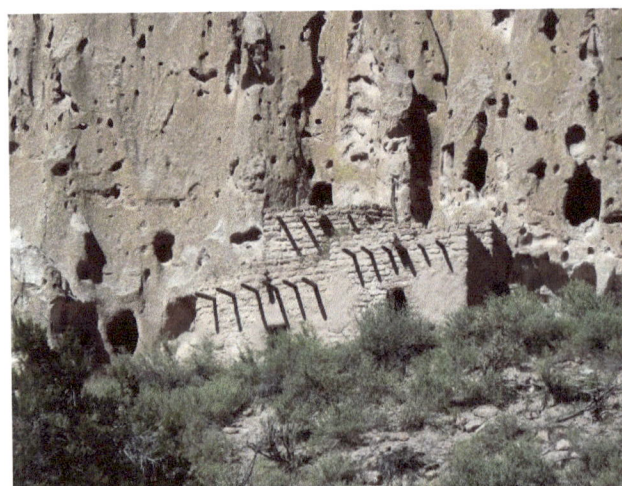

Bandalier National Monument, NM

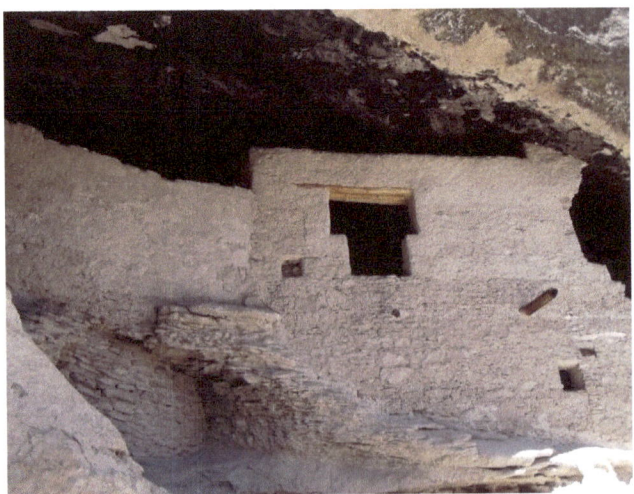

Gila Cliff Dwellings, NM

Beach Houses

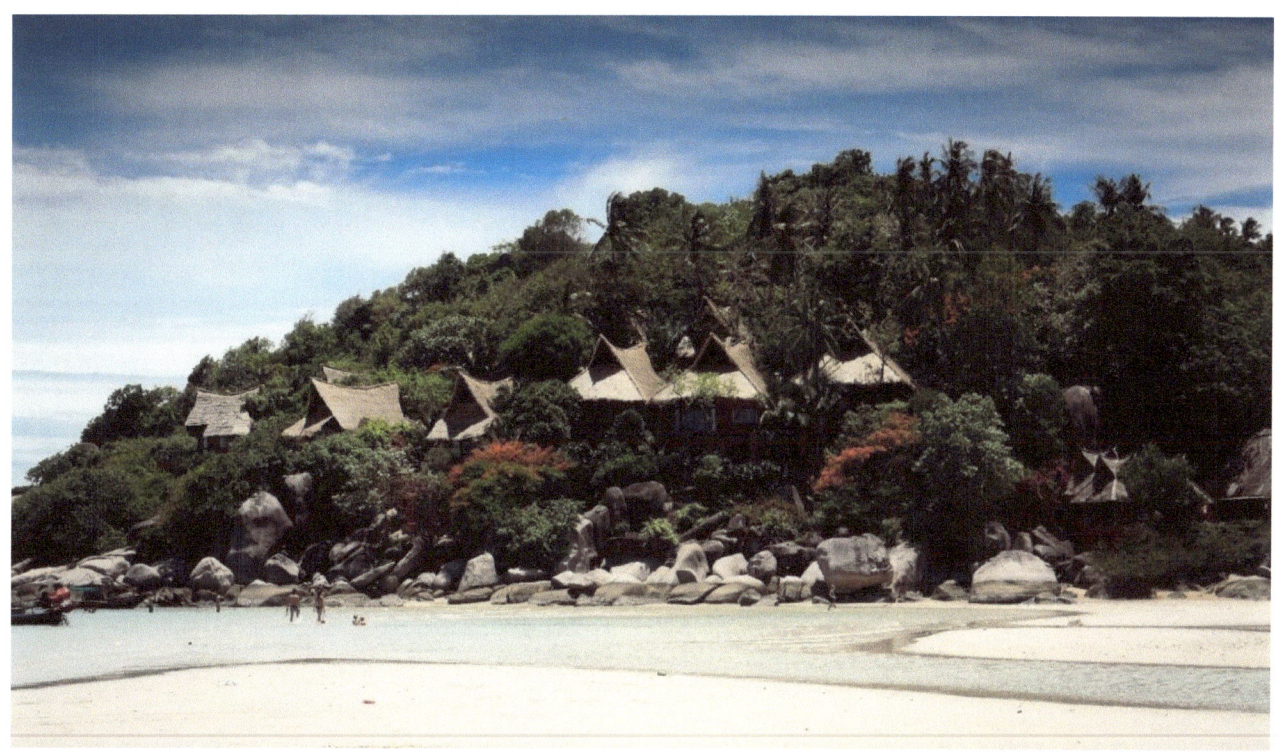

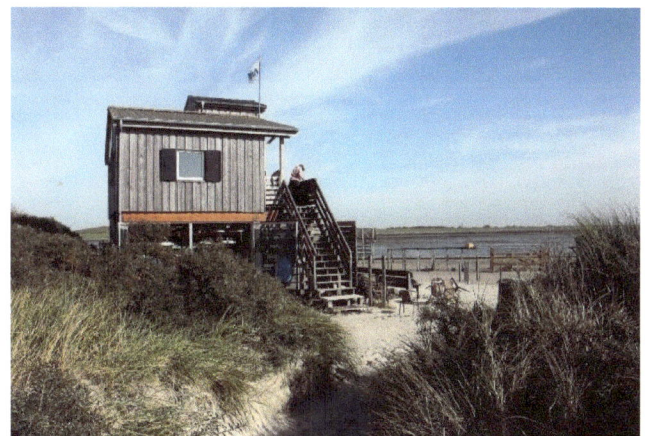

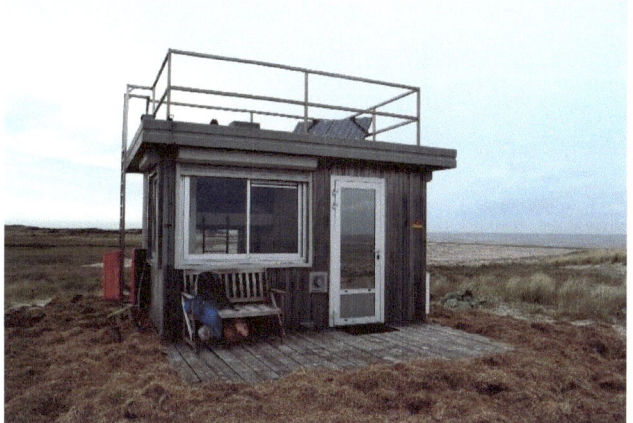

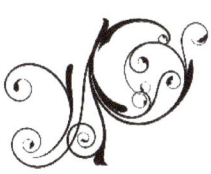

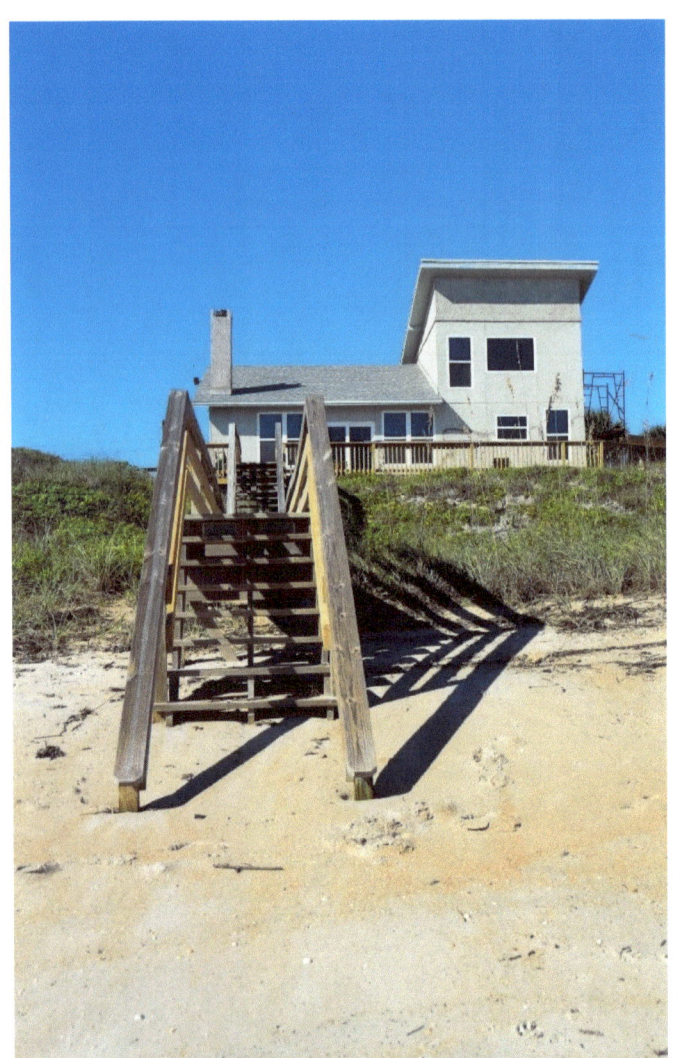
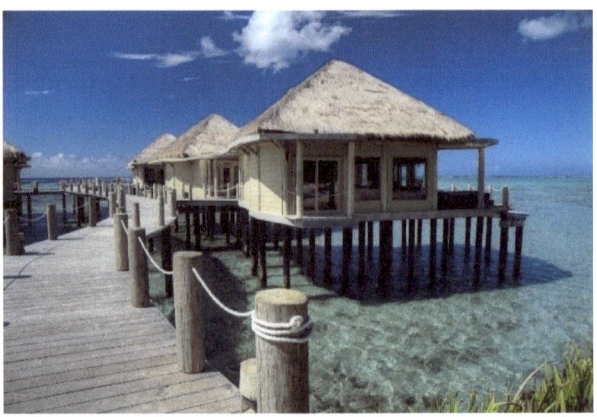
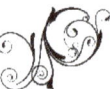
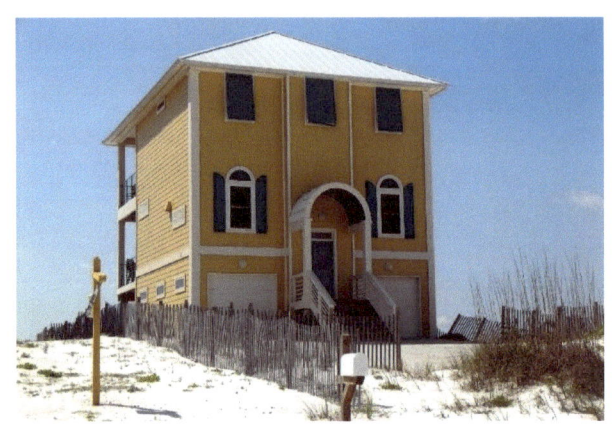
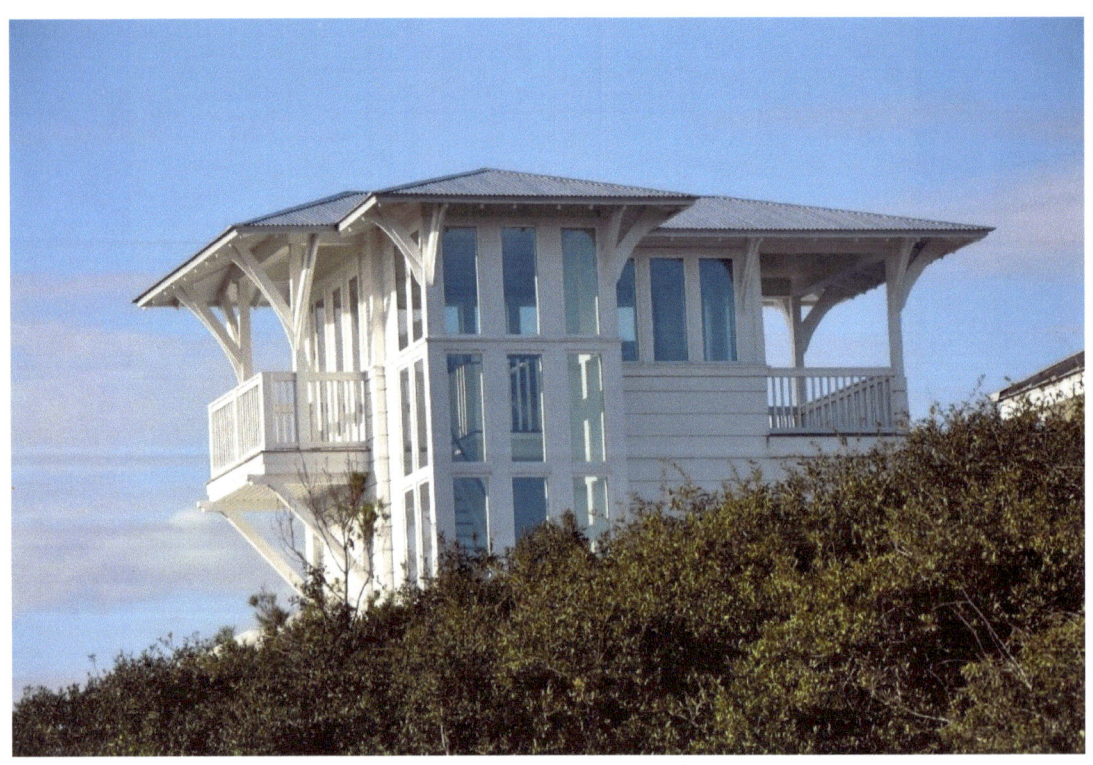

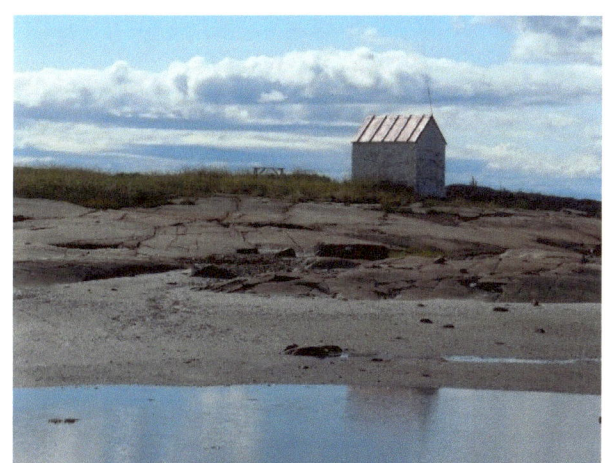
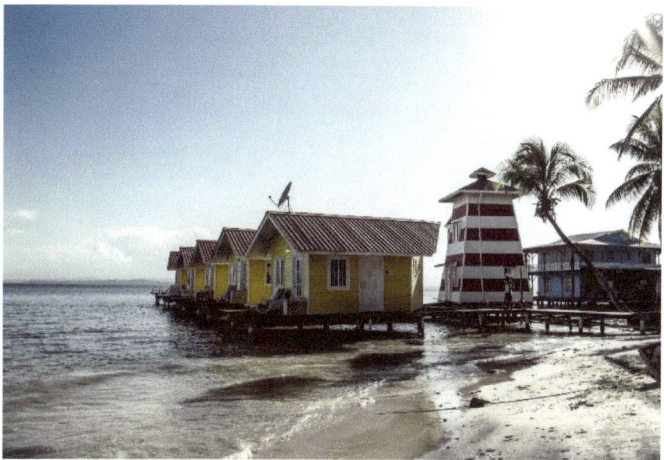
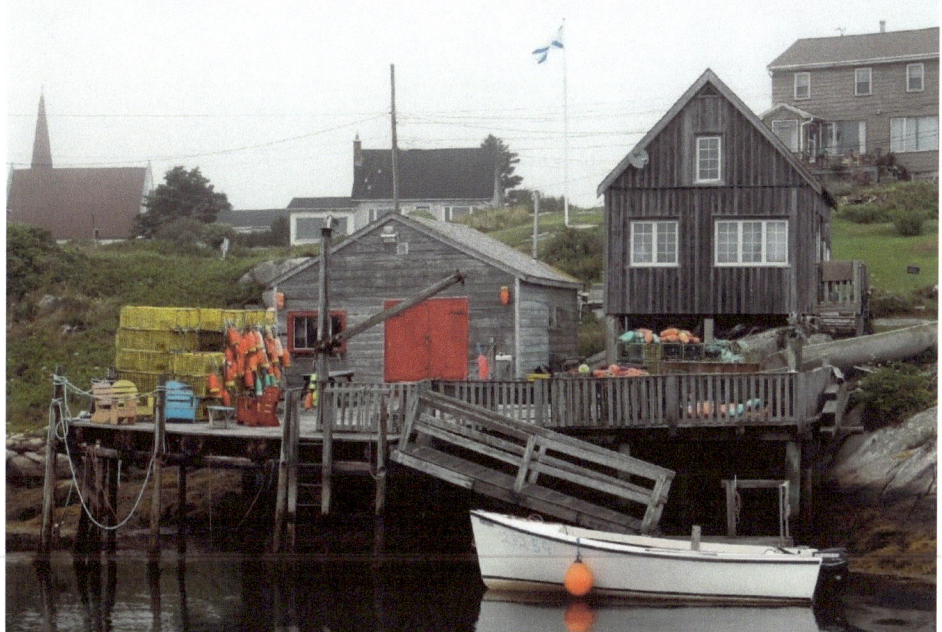

Peggy's Cove, Nova Scotia

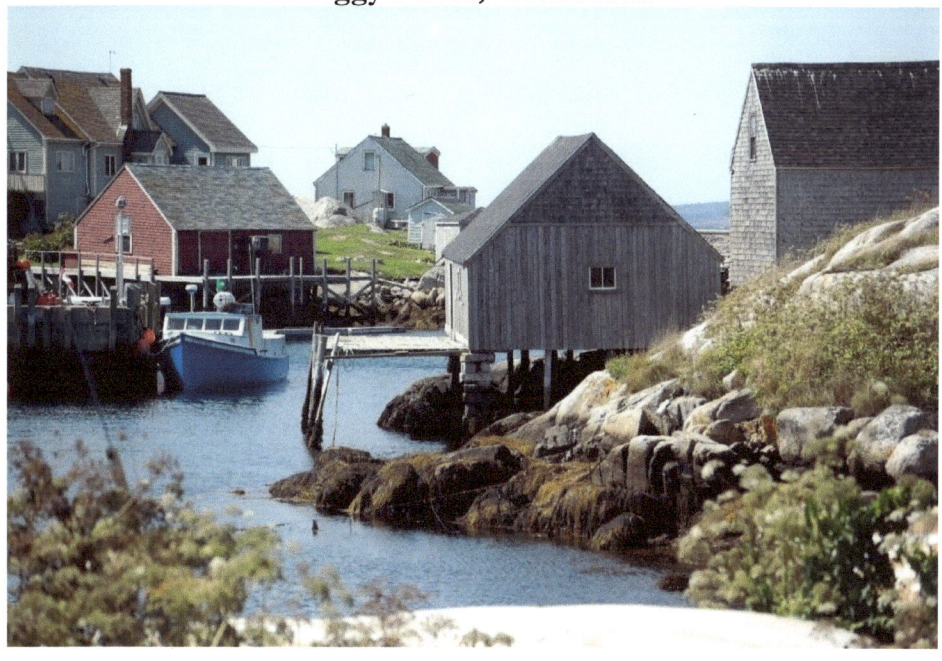

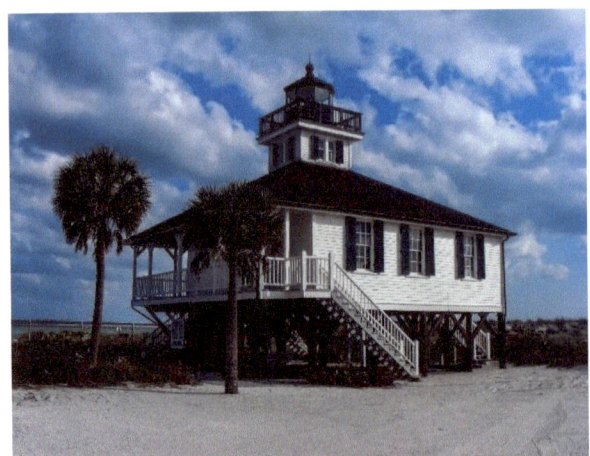
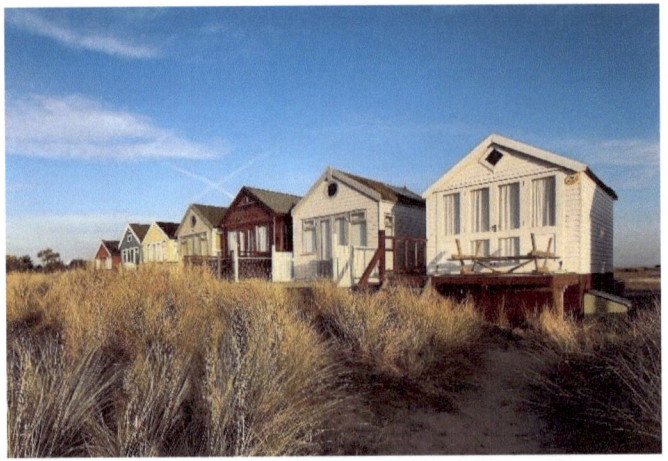
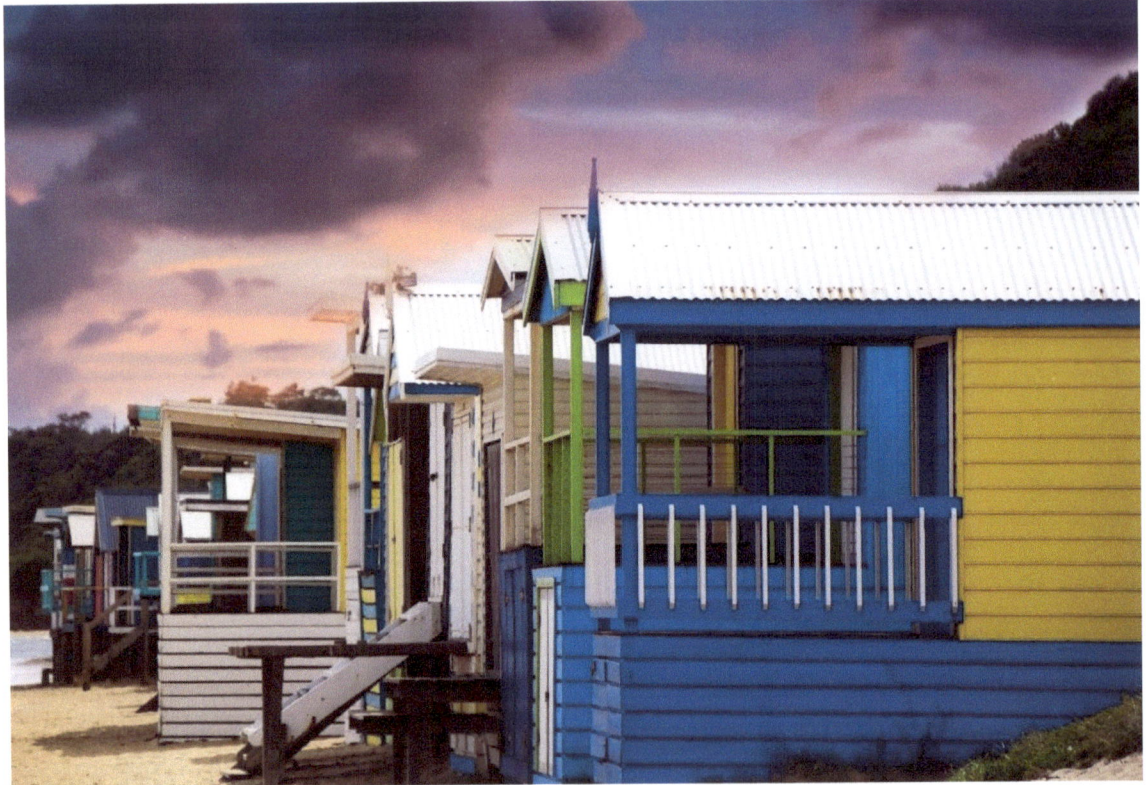
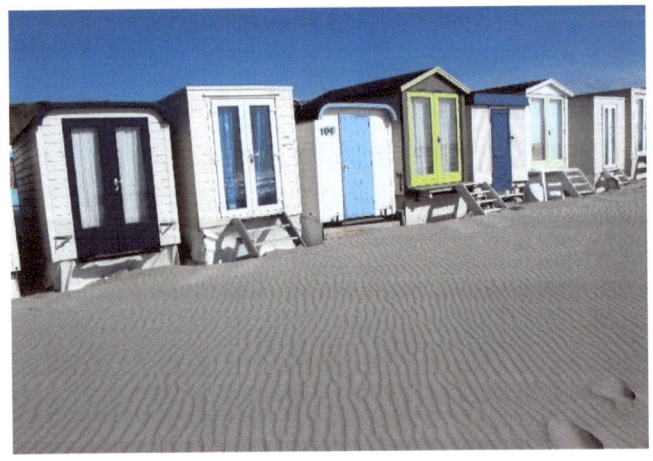
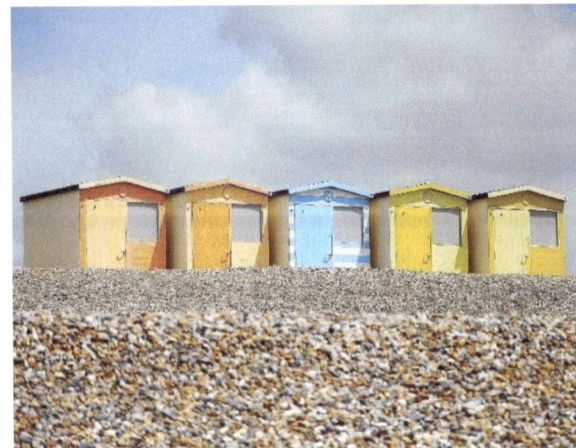

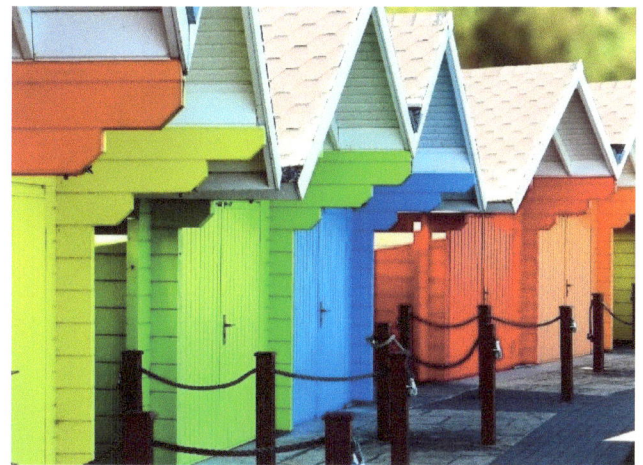
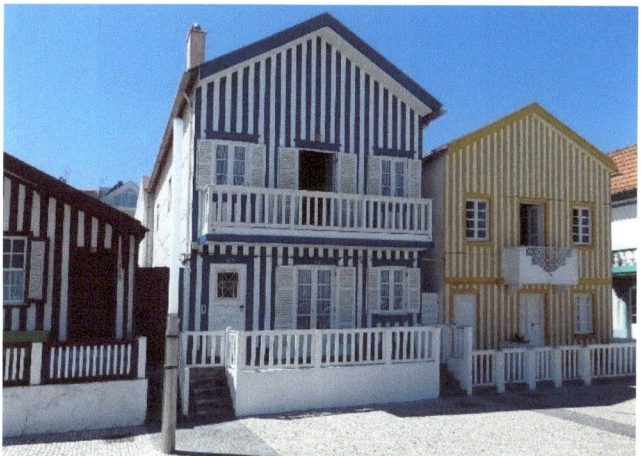
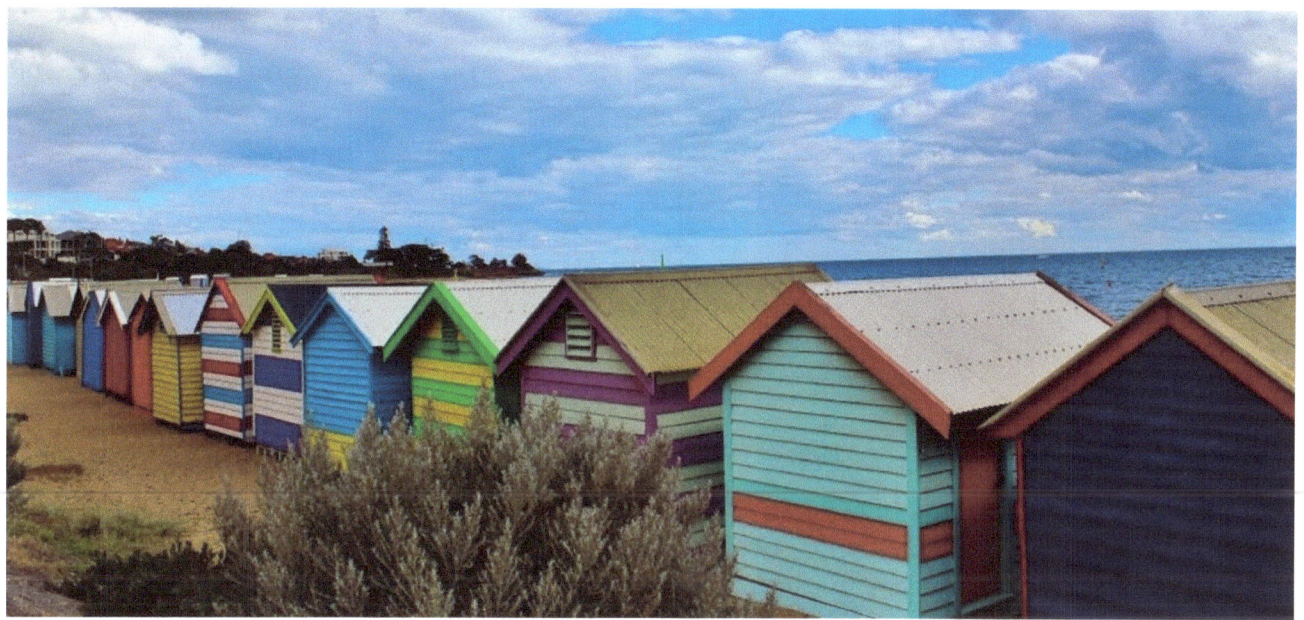
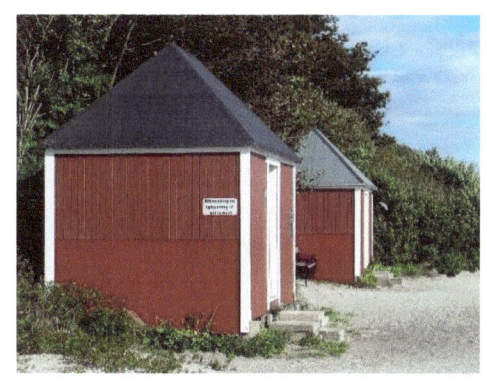
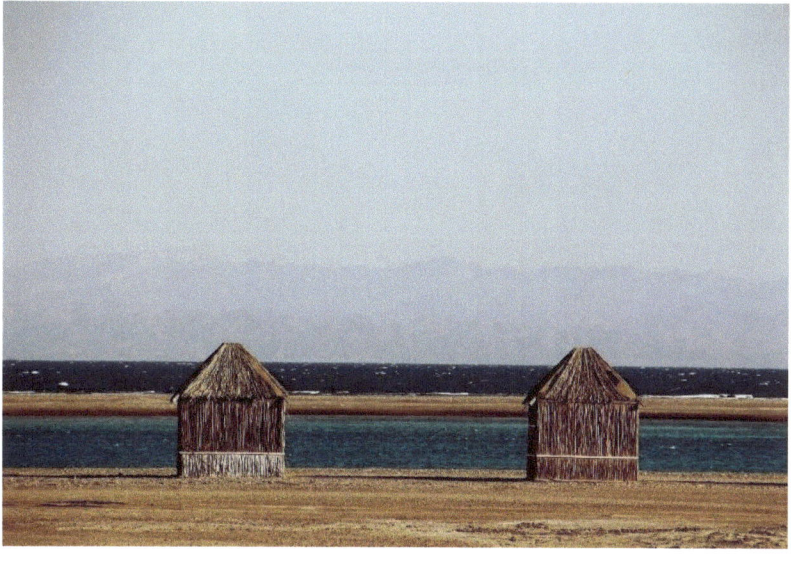

Boathouses

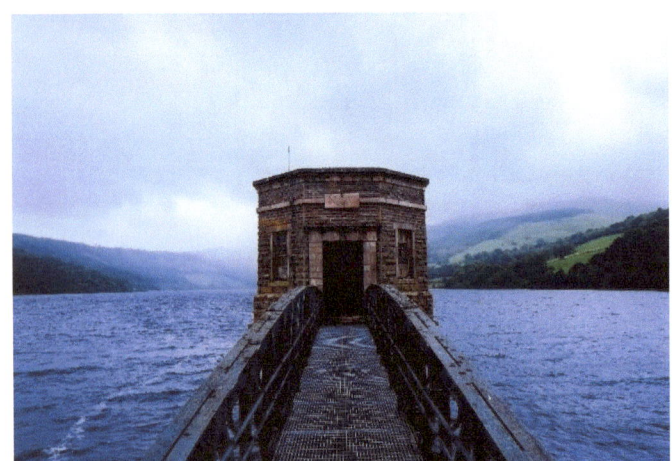
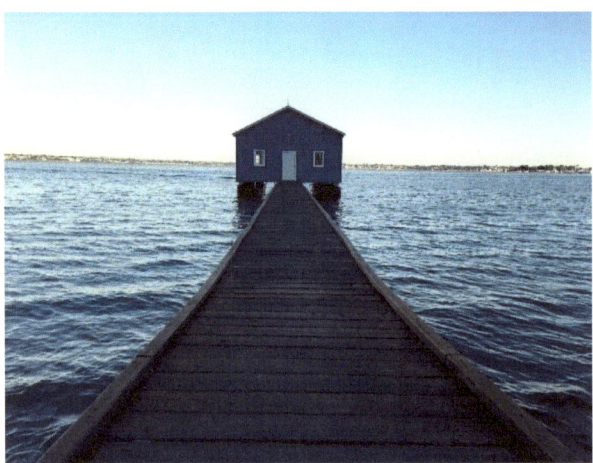
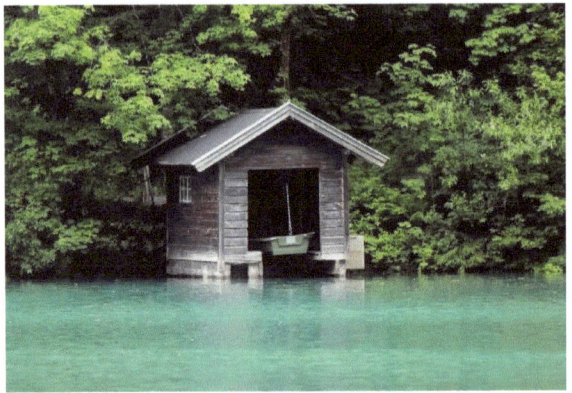
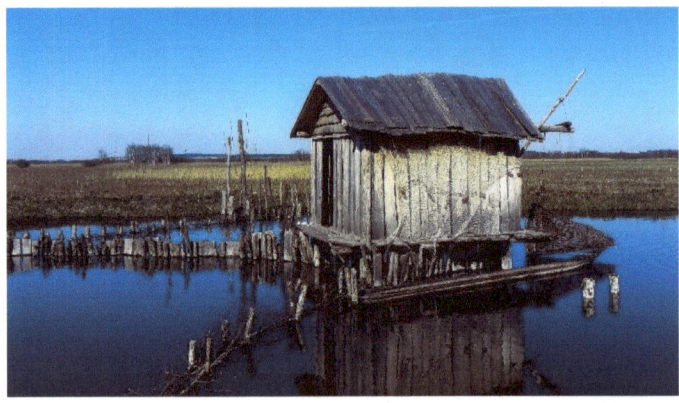
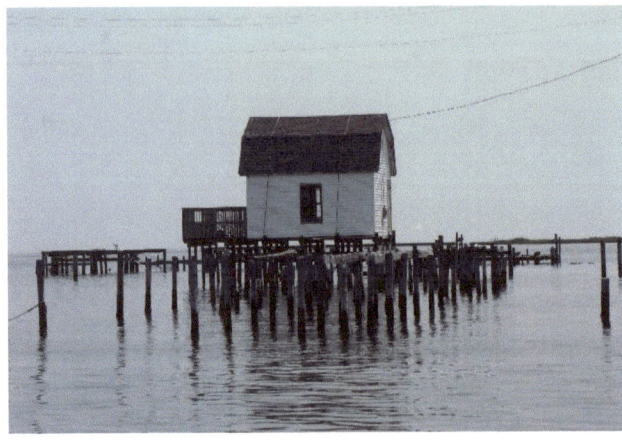
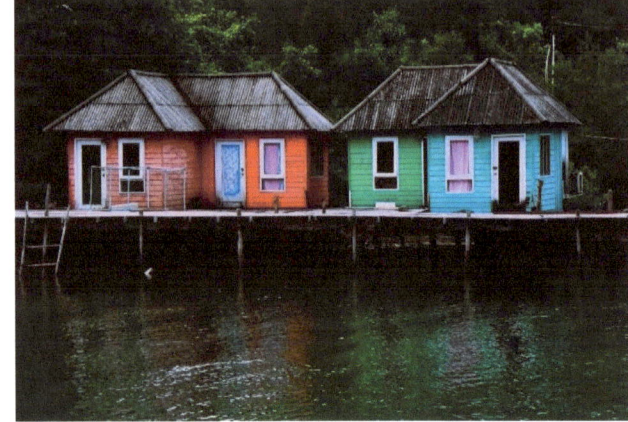

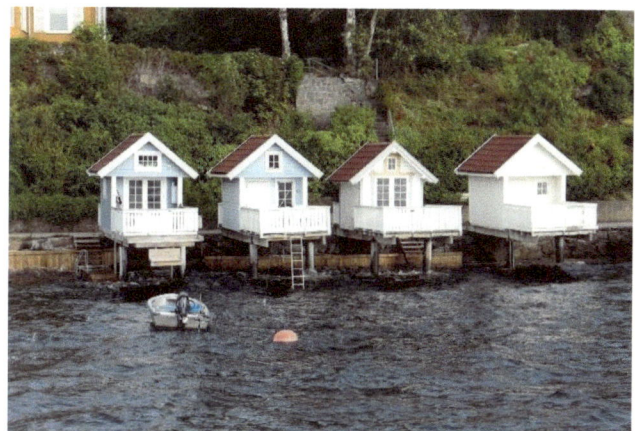
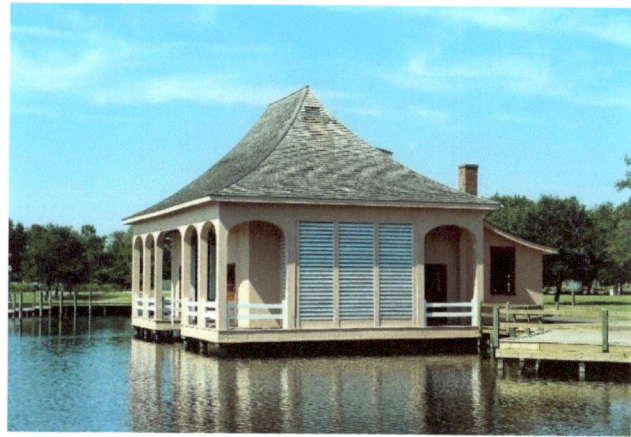
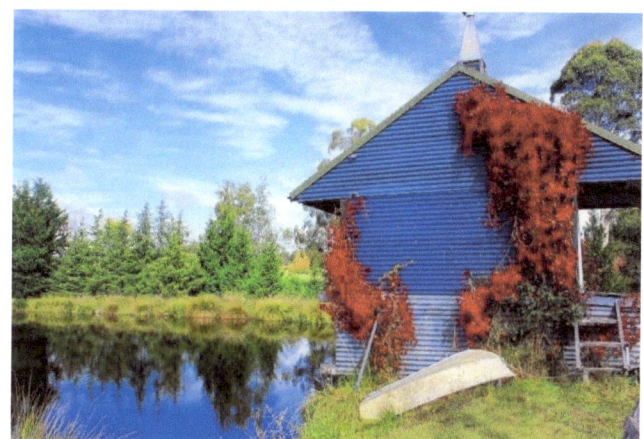
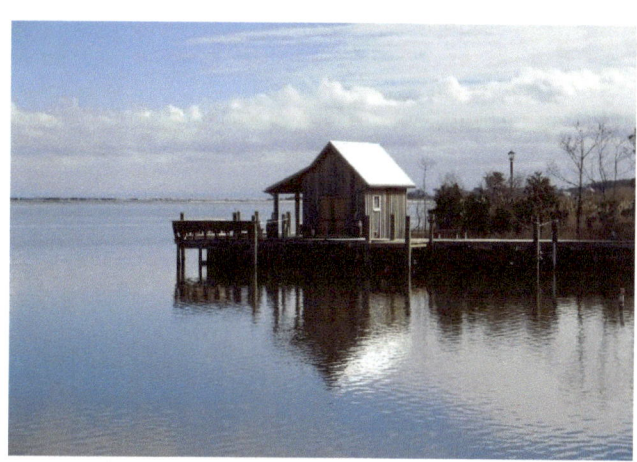
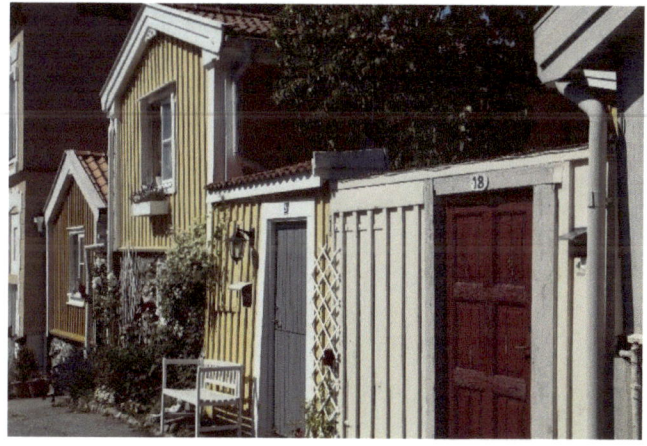
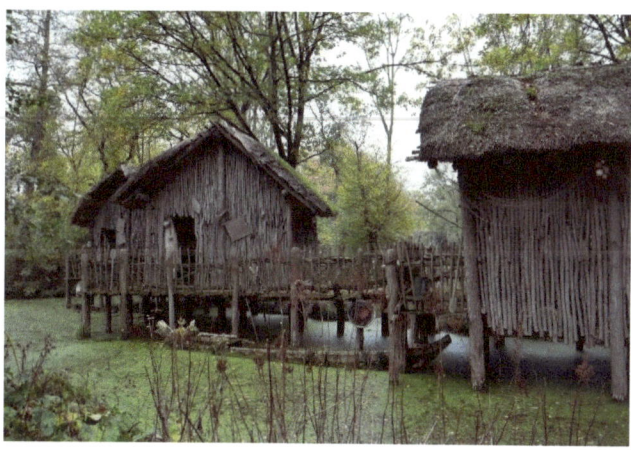
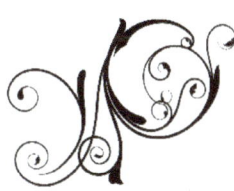

Houseboats

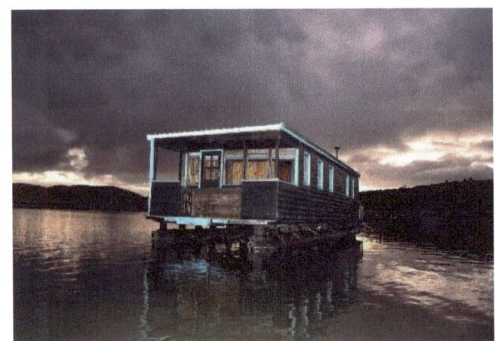
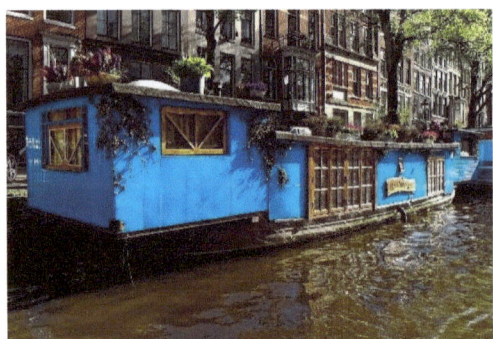
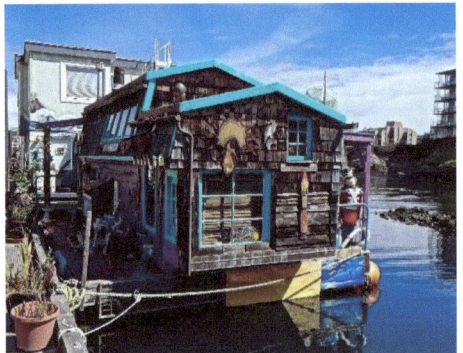
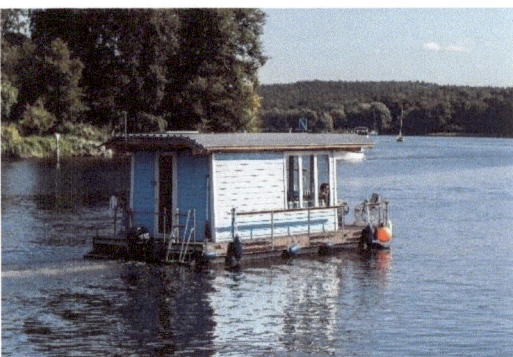
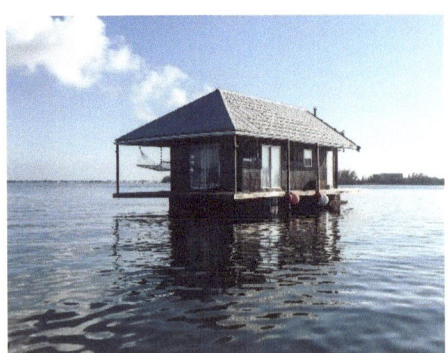
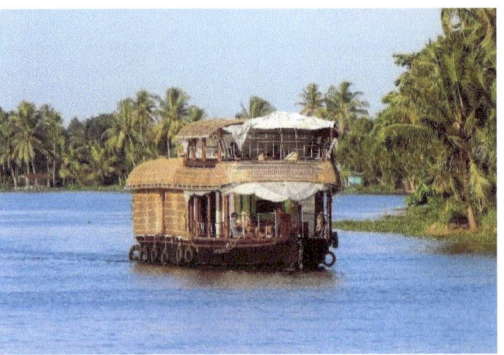
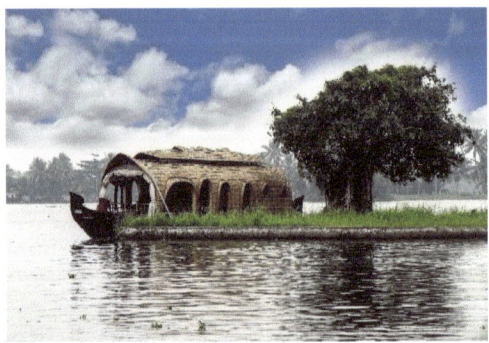
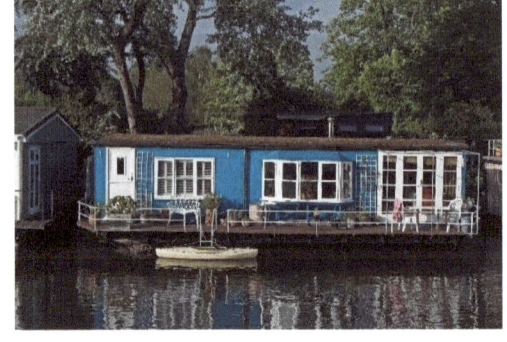

Desert Dwellings & Mud Huts

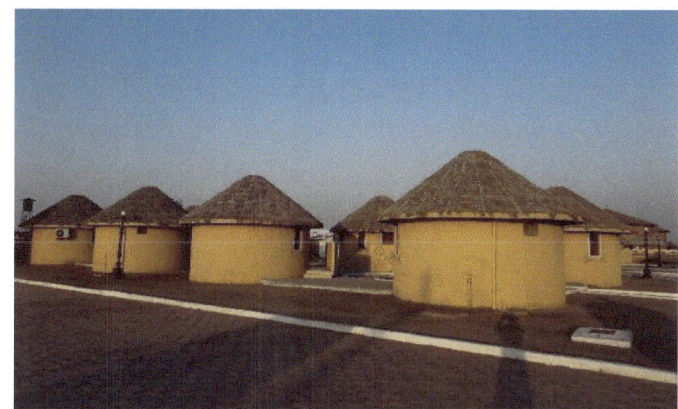
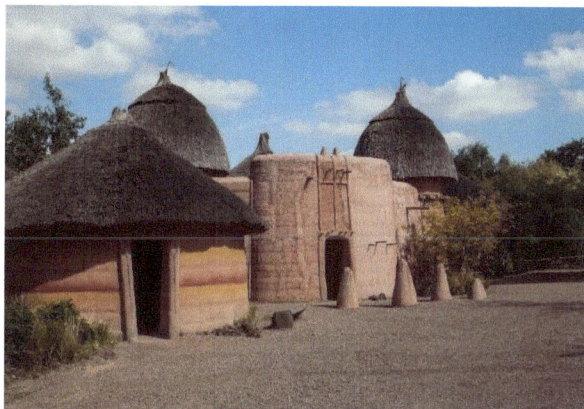
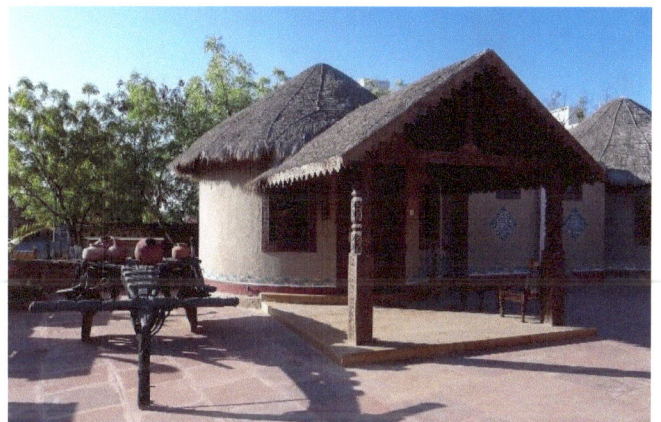
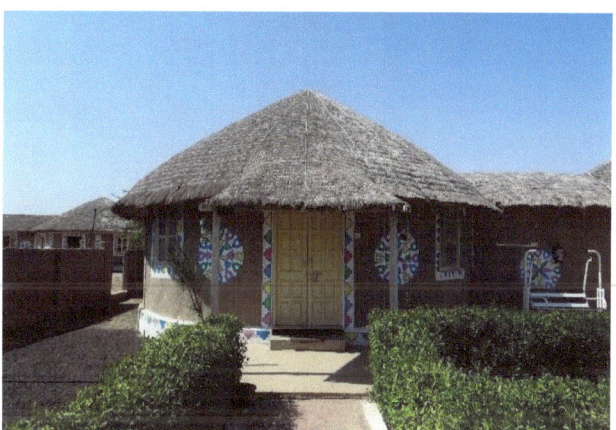

Bhunga

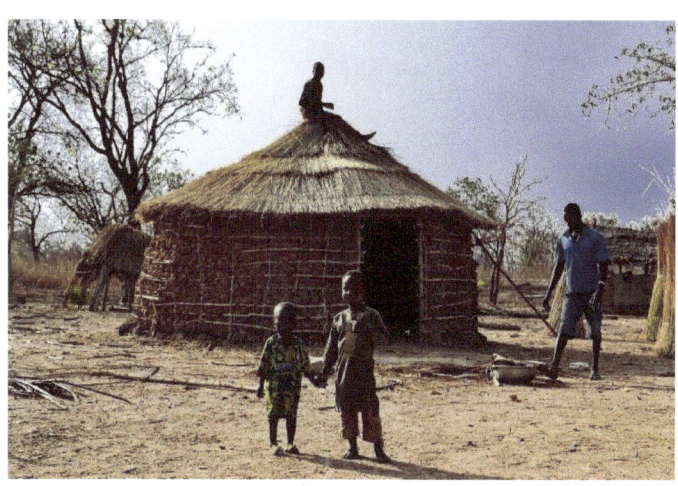

Ghana

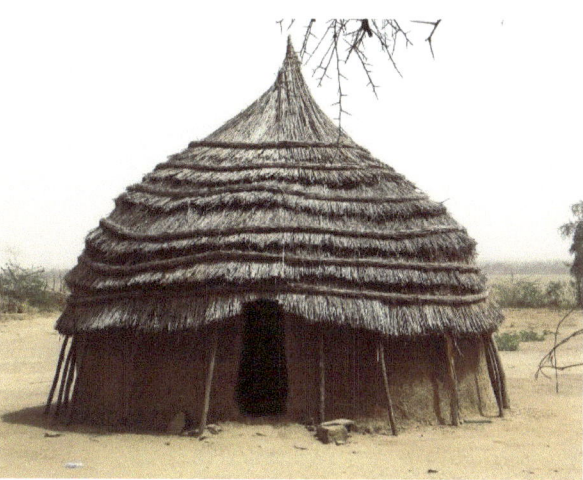

Niger

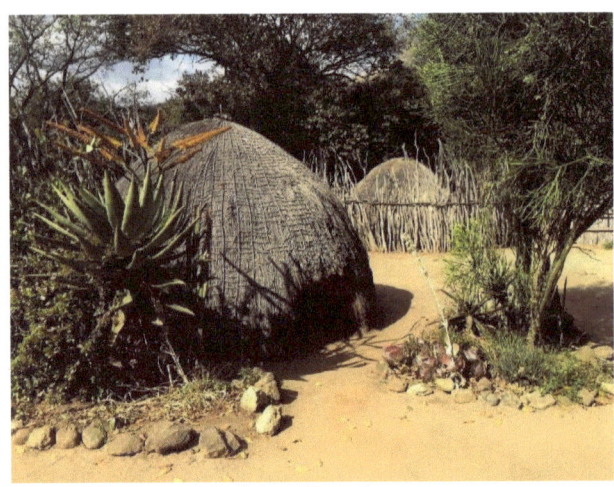

Swaziland

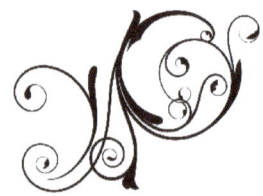

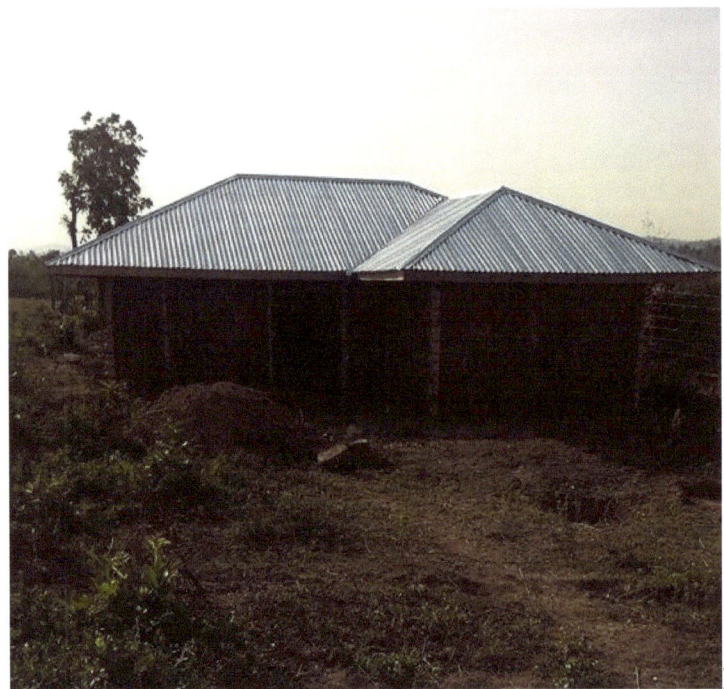

Homa Bay, Kenya

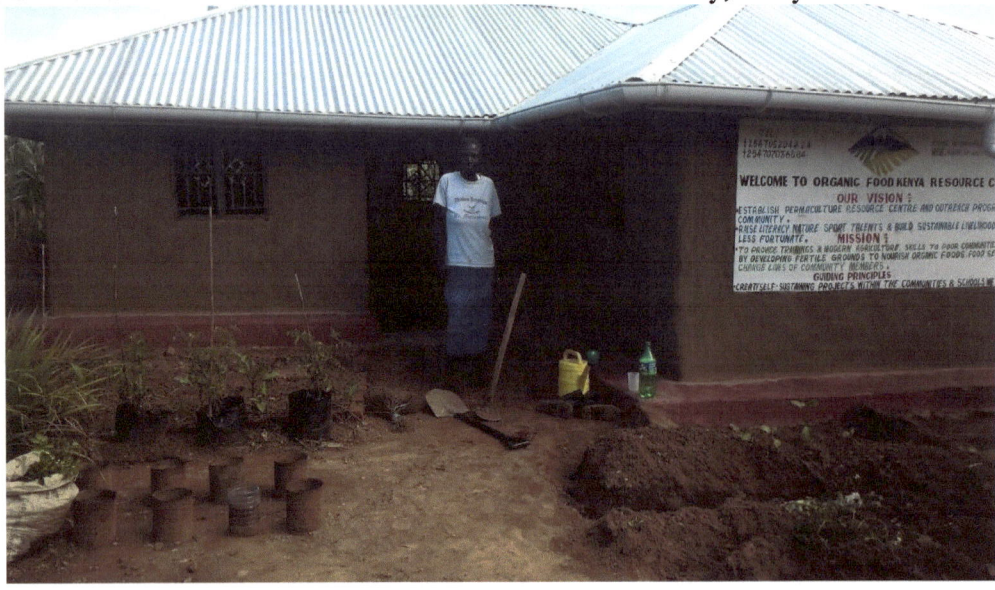

Solar

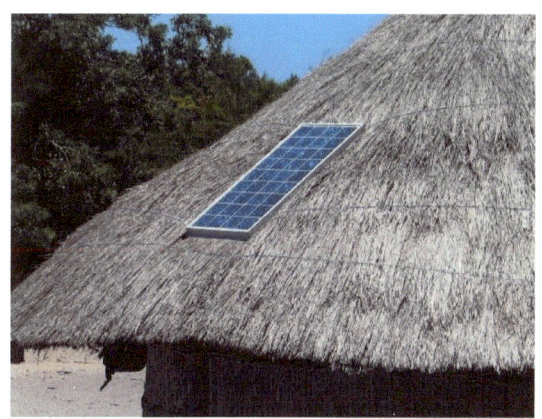
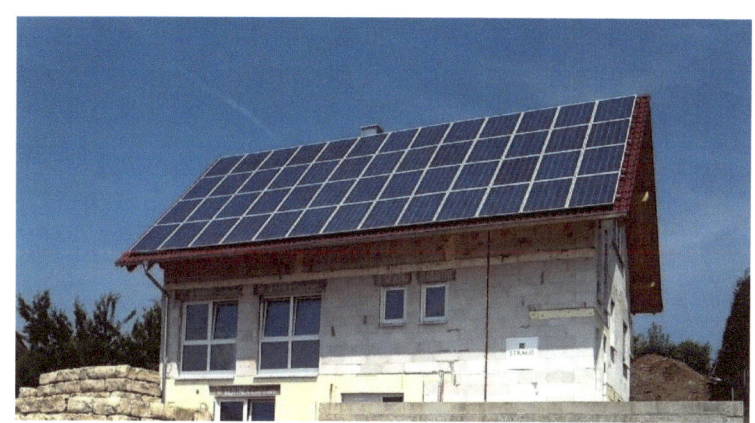

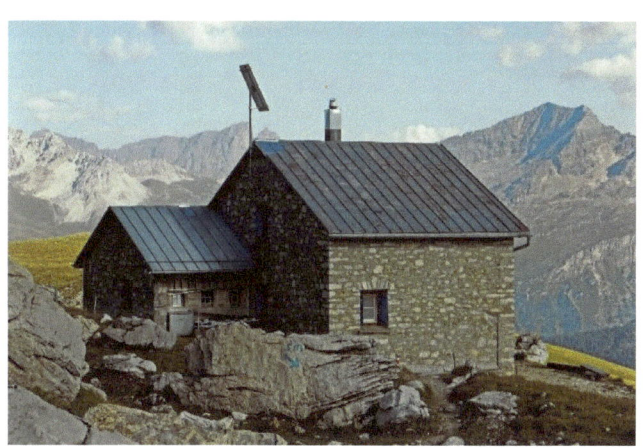
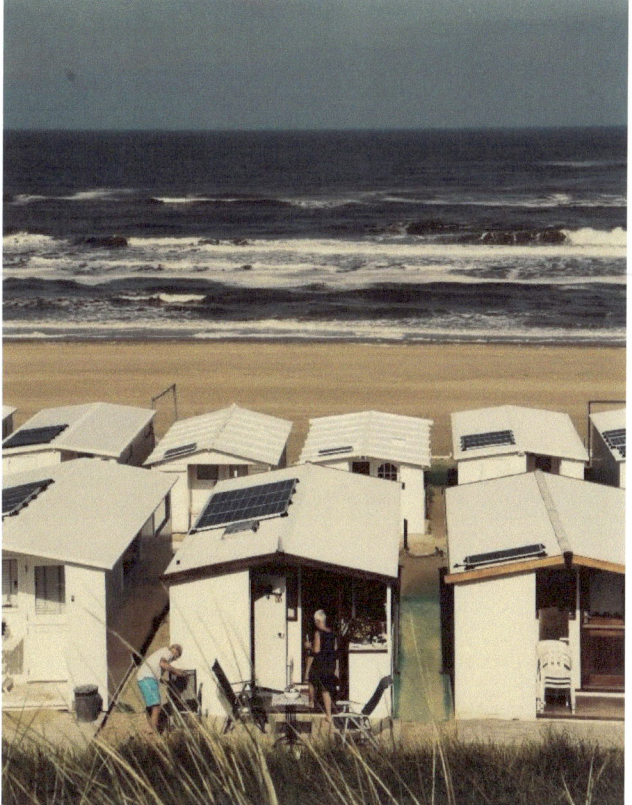

Piers & Stilts

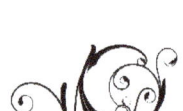

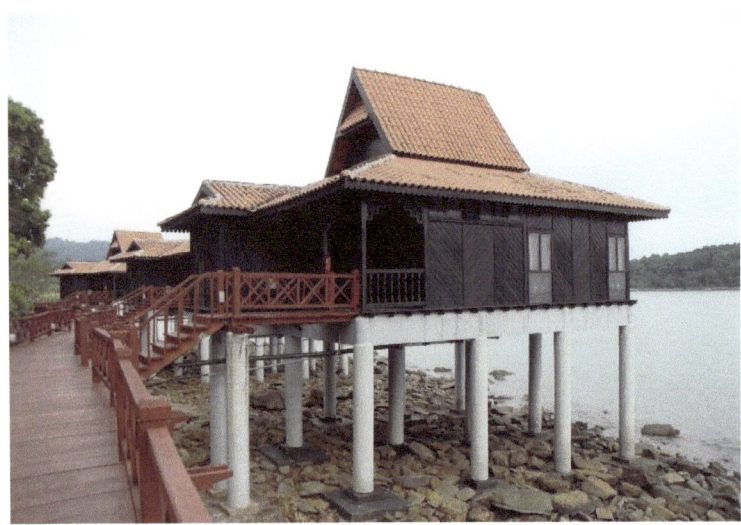

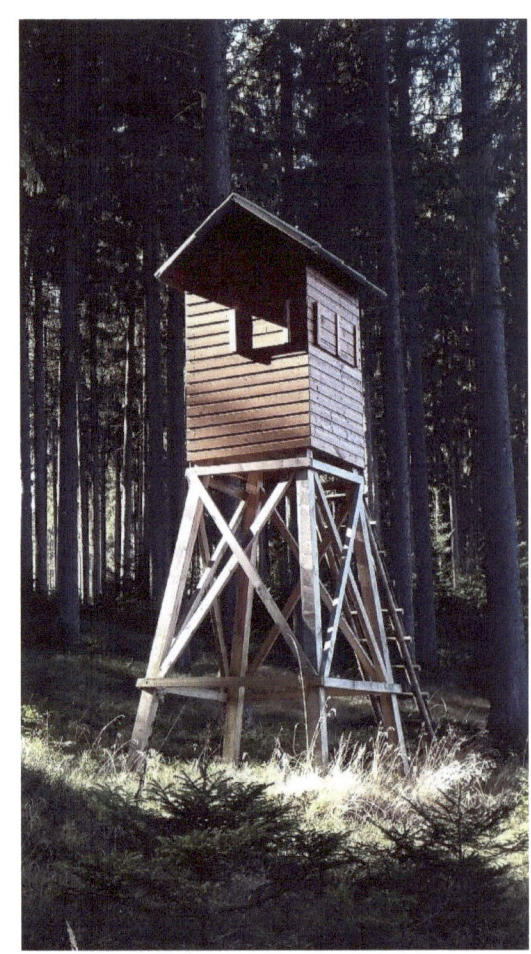

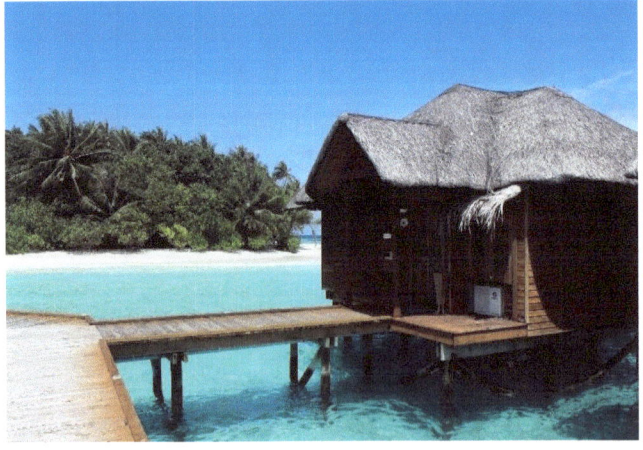

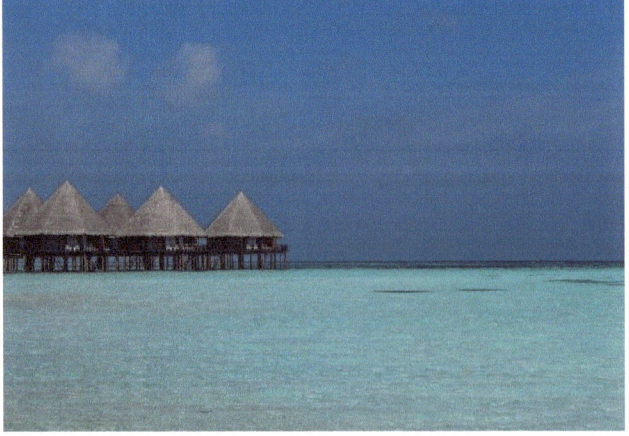

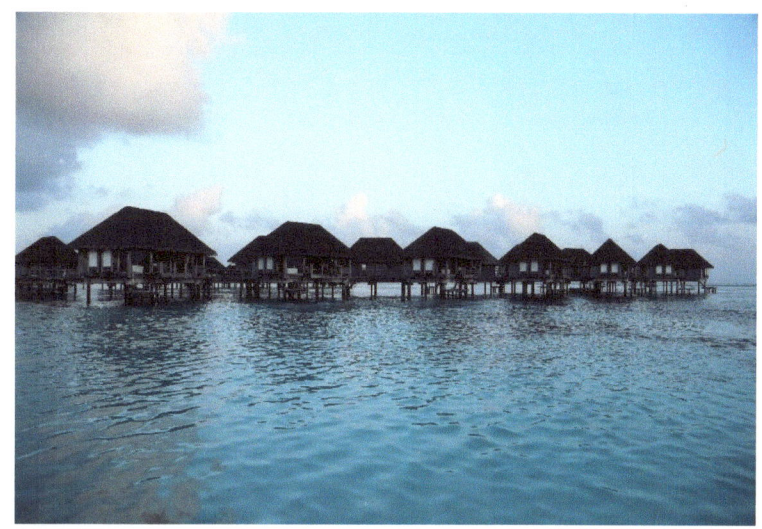

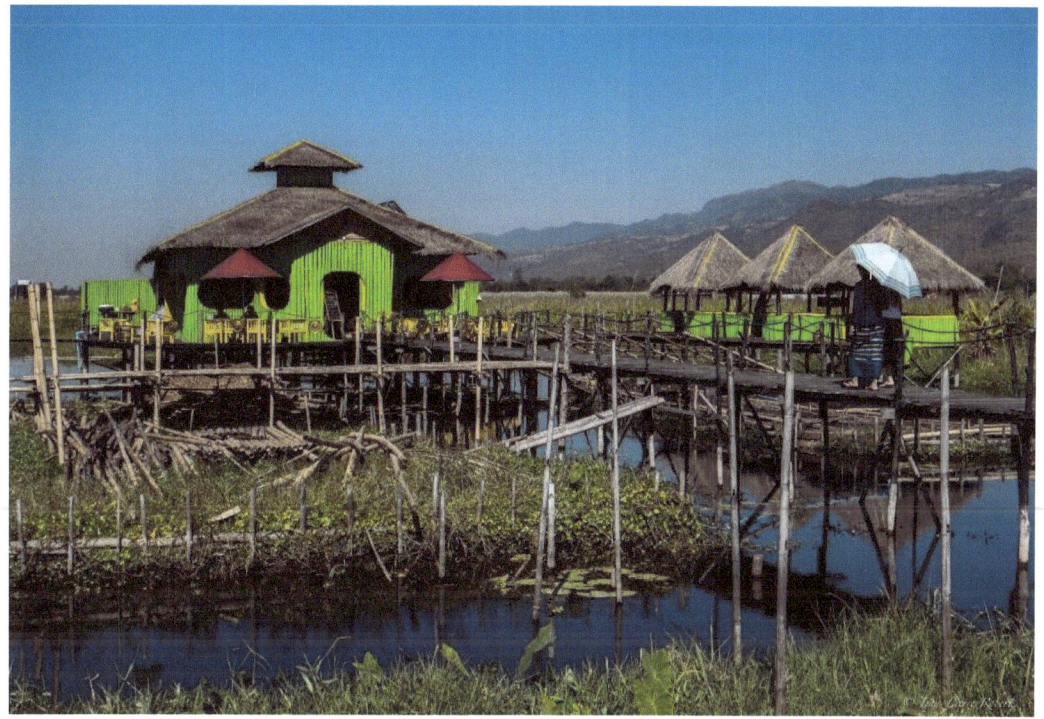

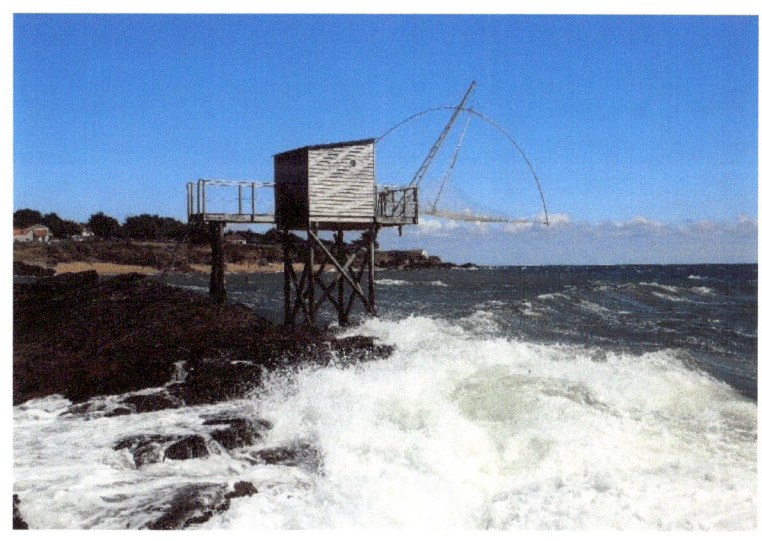

Towers

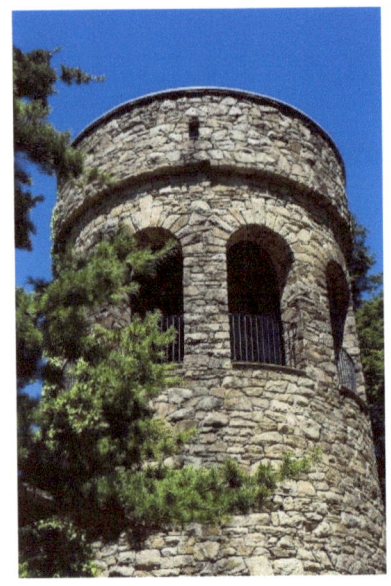
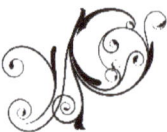
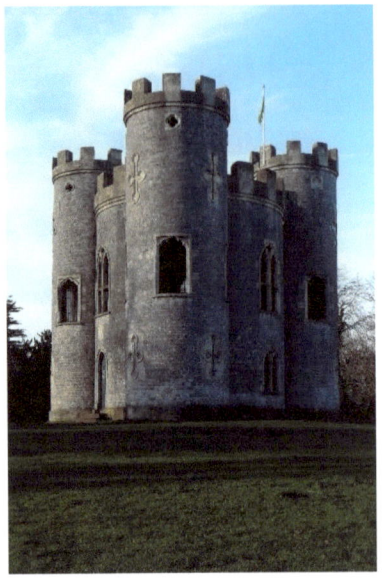
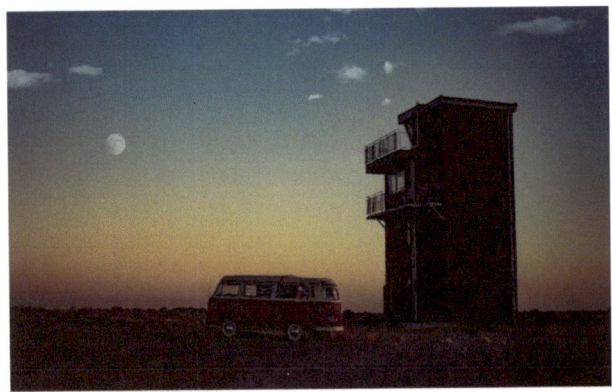
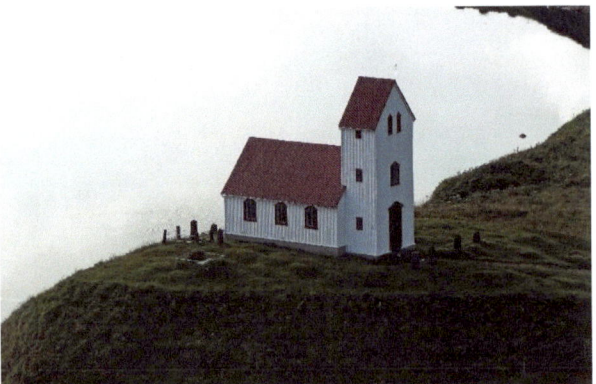
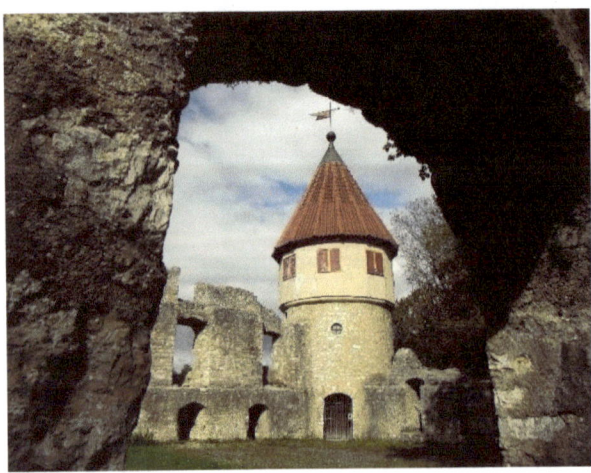
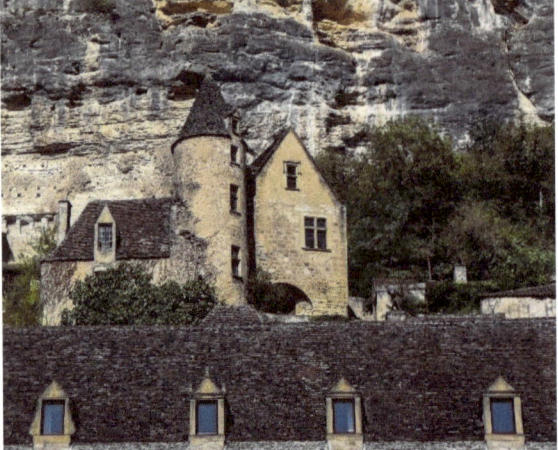

BEST OF TINY HOUSE PHOTOBOOK

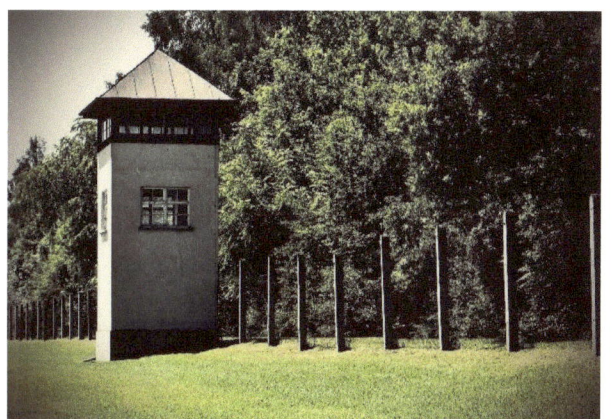
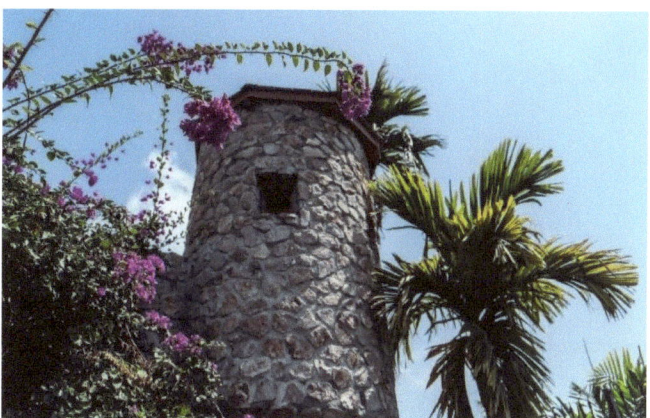

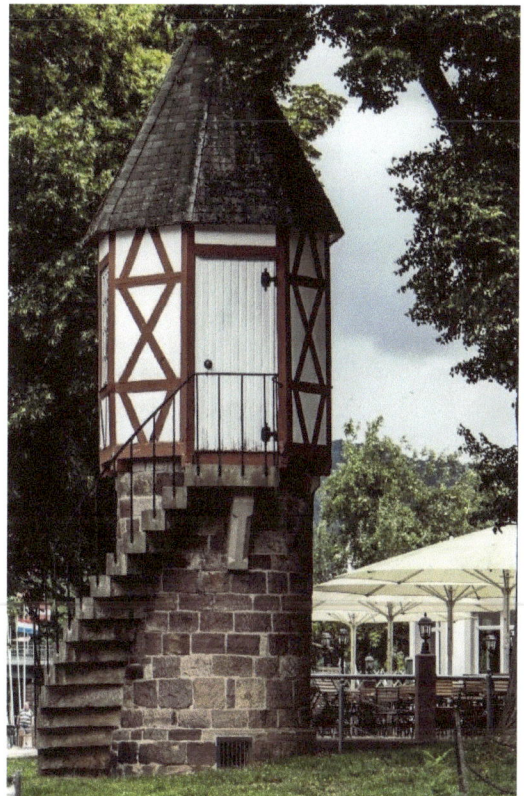

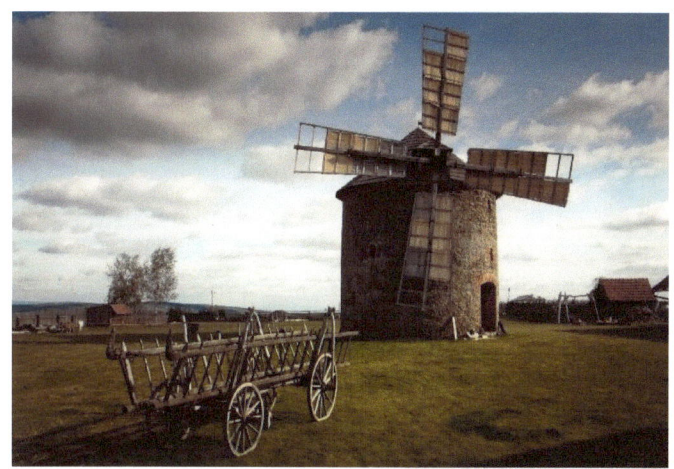
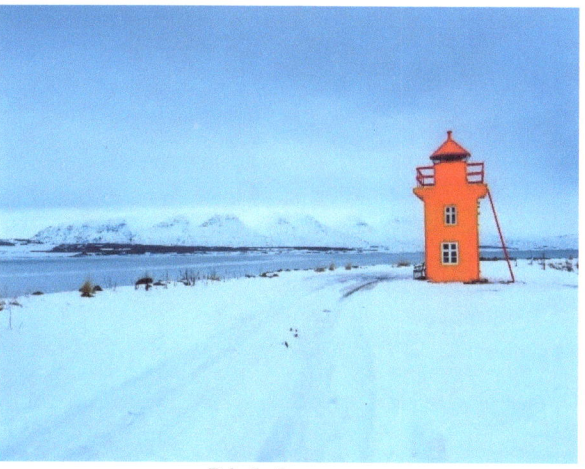

Lighthouse

Log Cabins

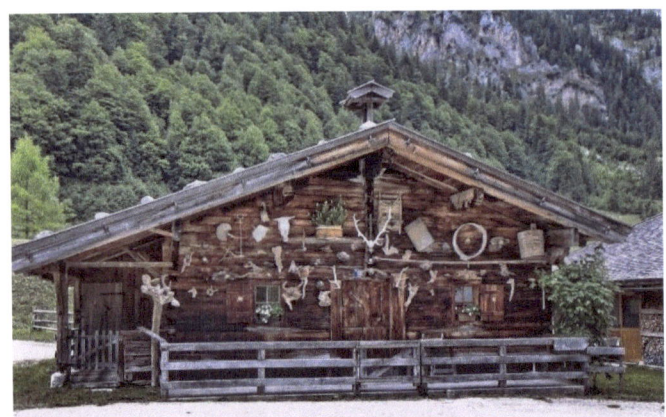
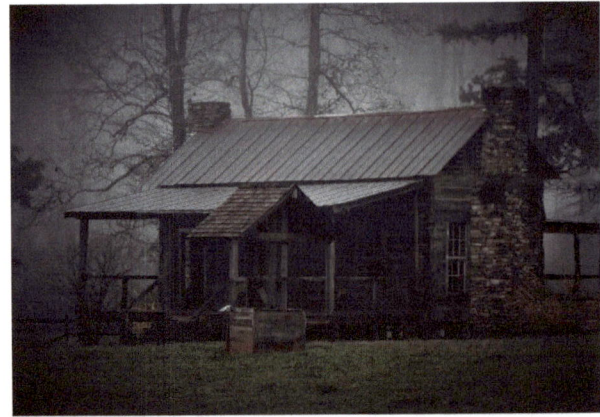
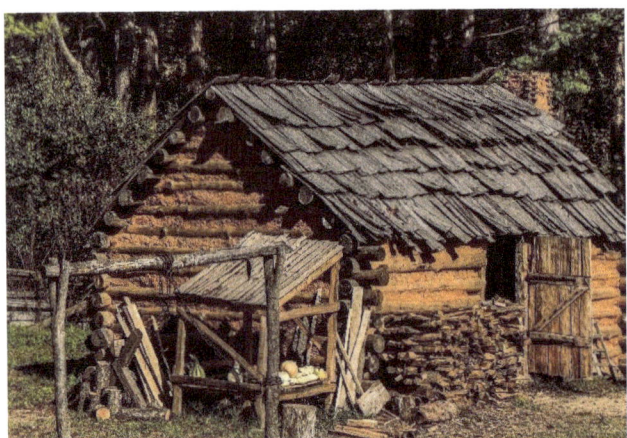
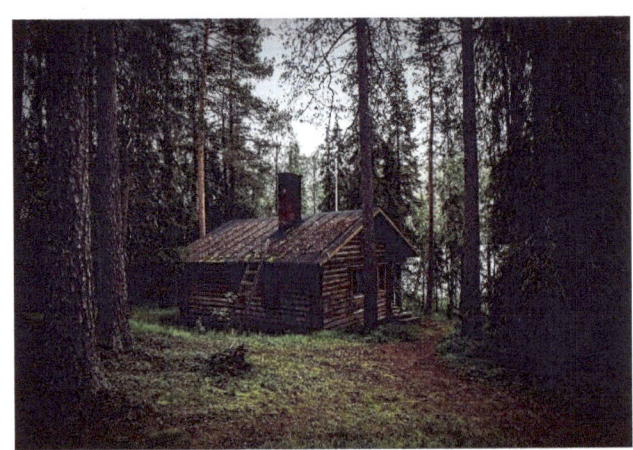
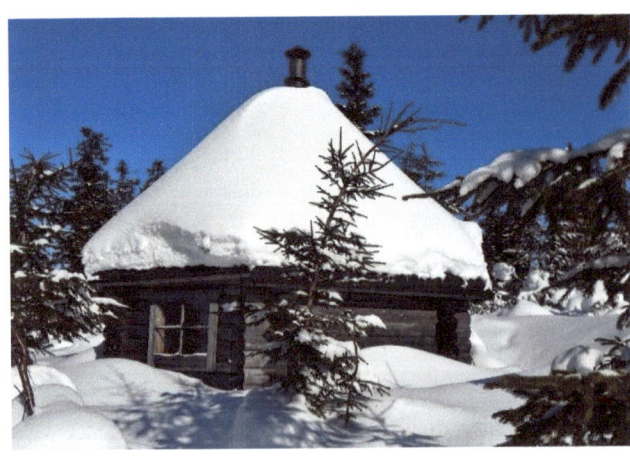
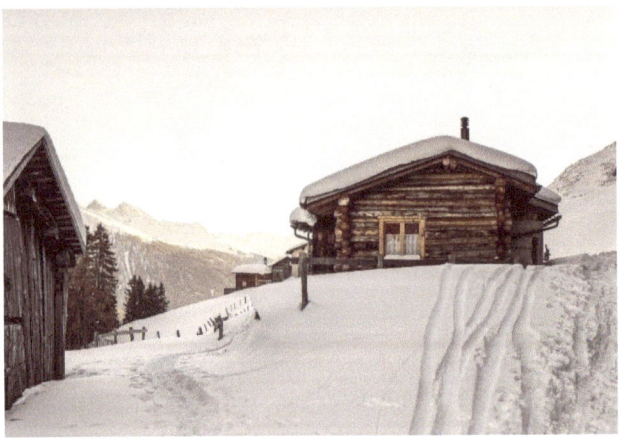

Wood Homes

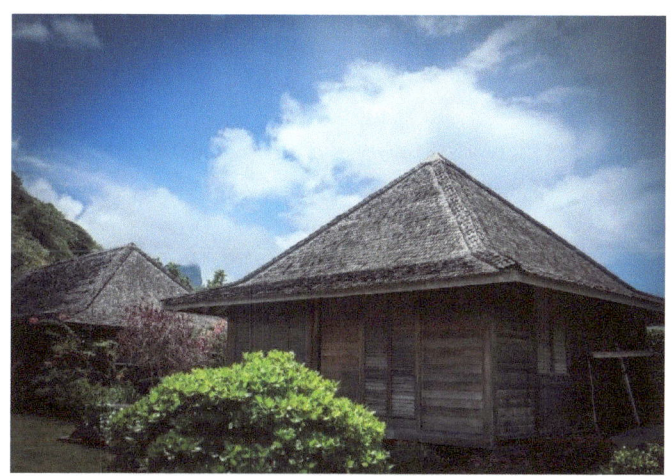
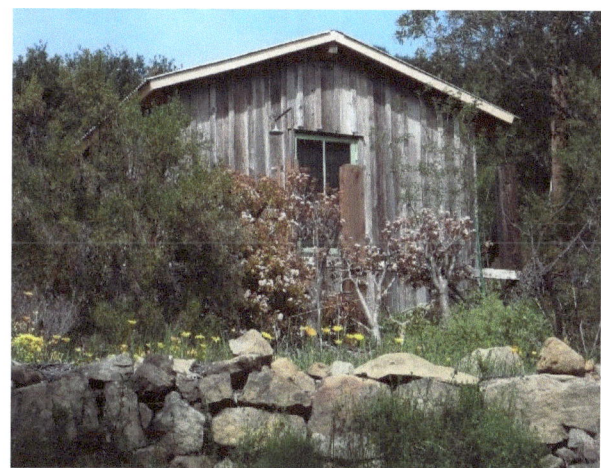
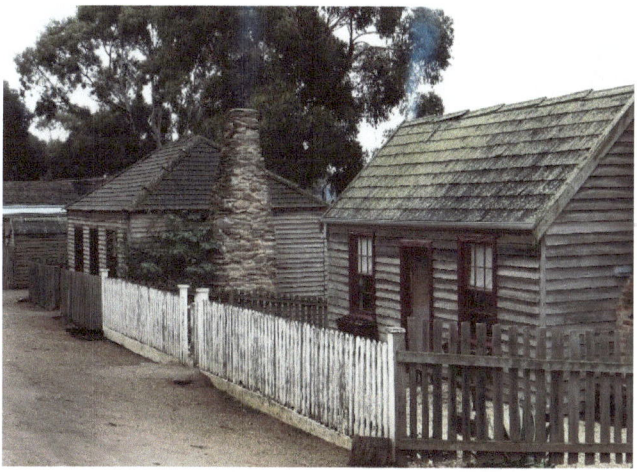
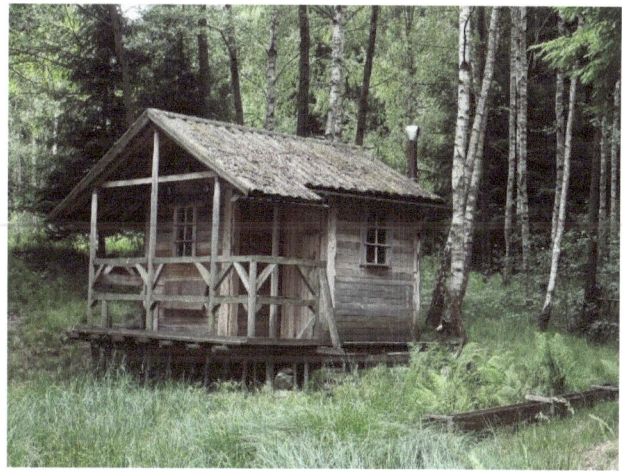
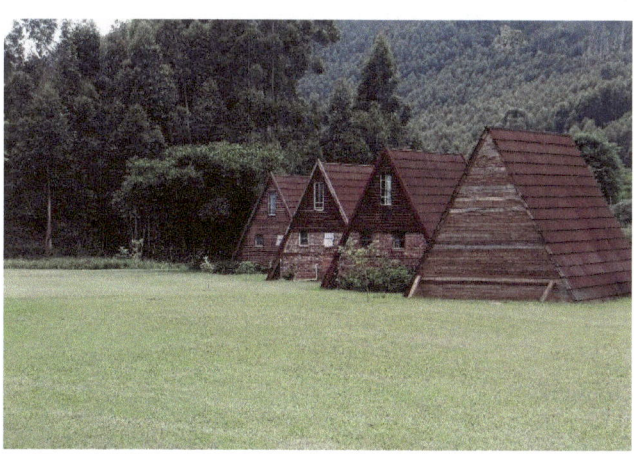
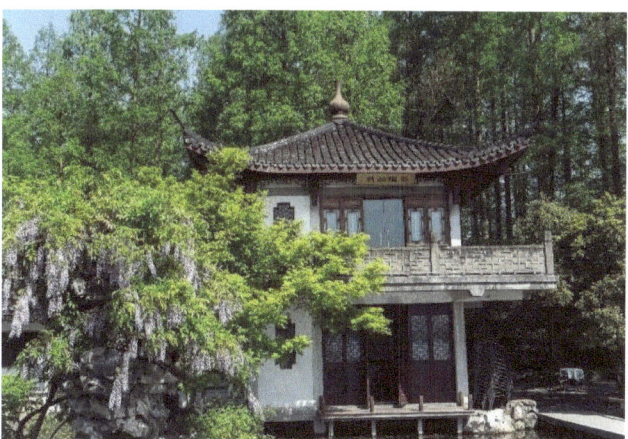

Bungalows

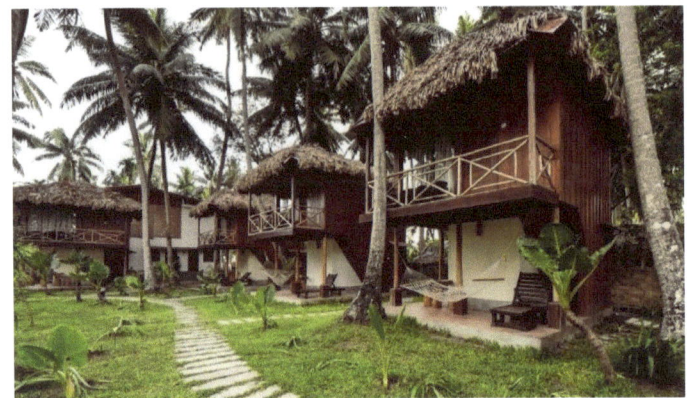
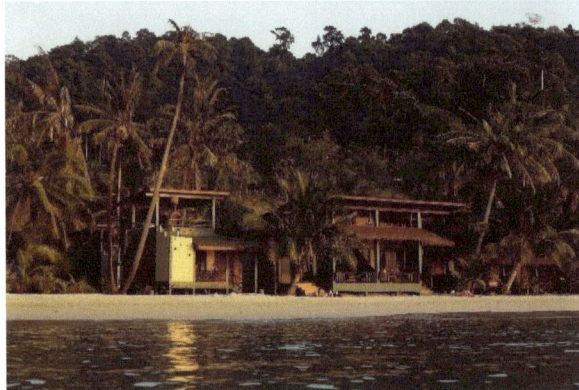
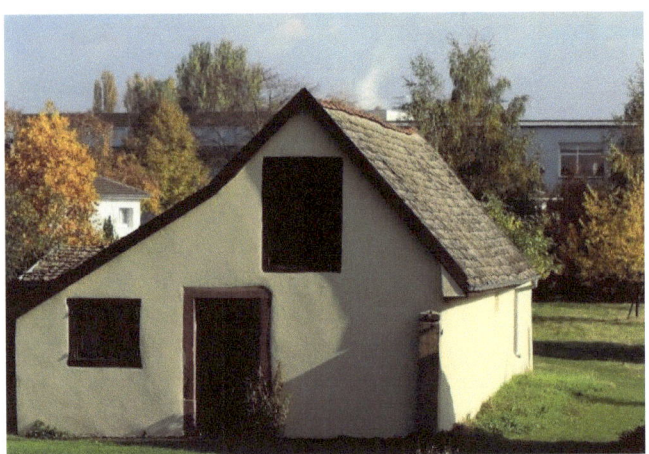
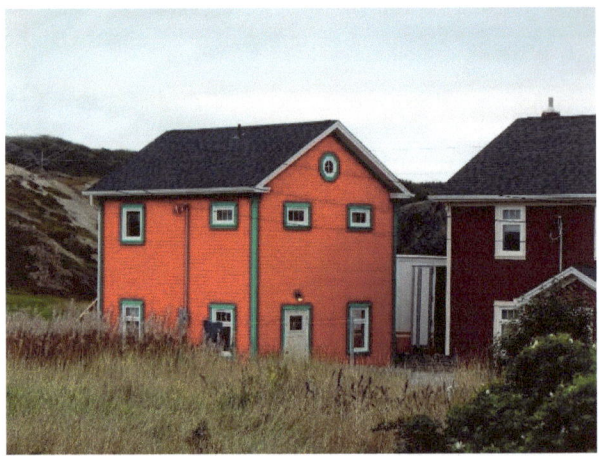
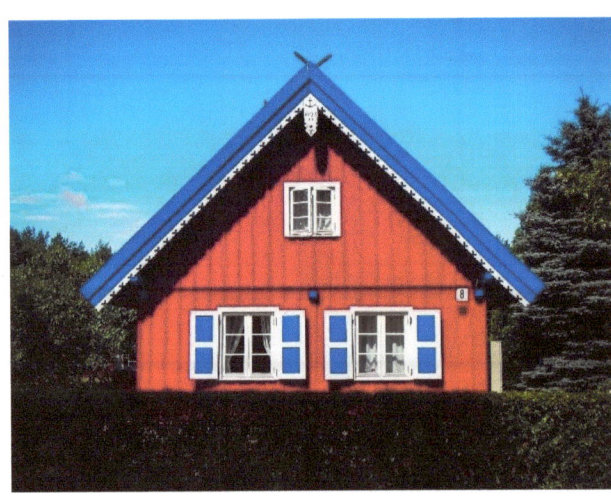
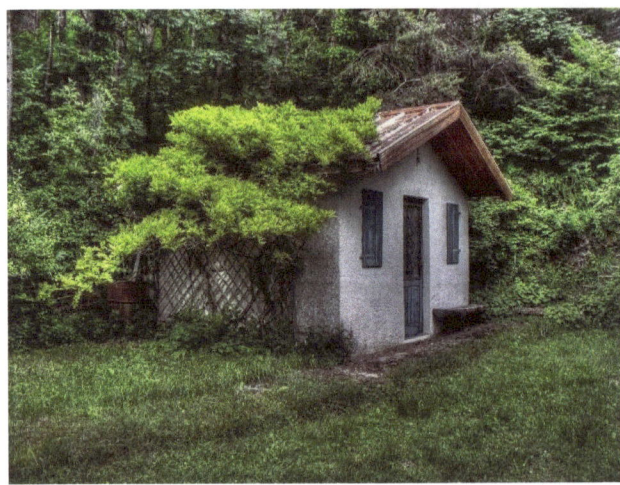

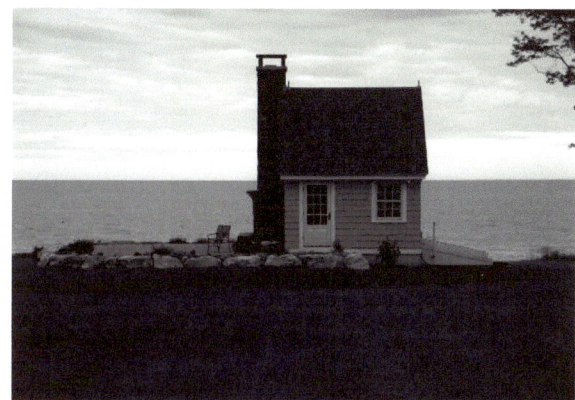
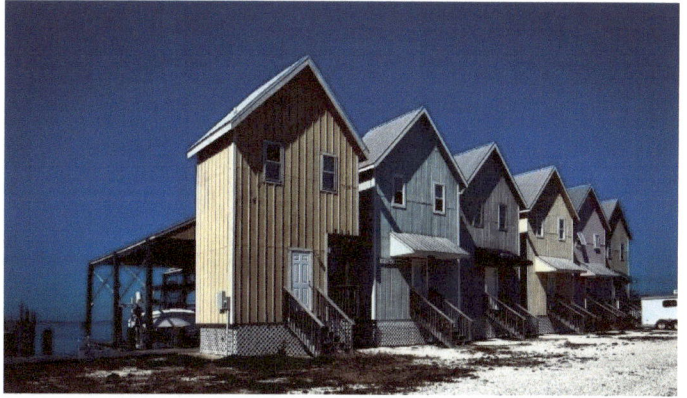
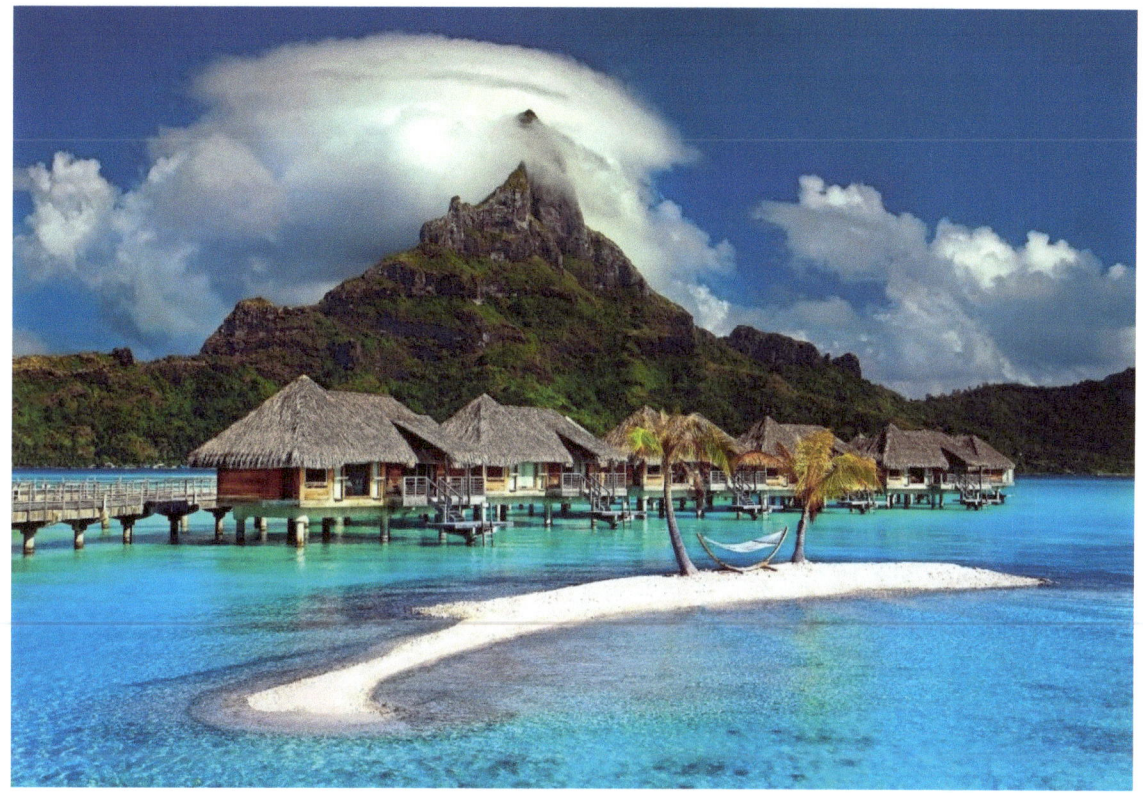
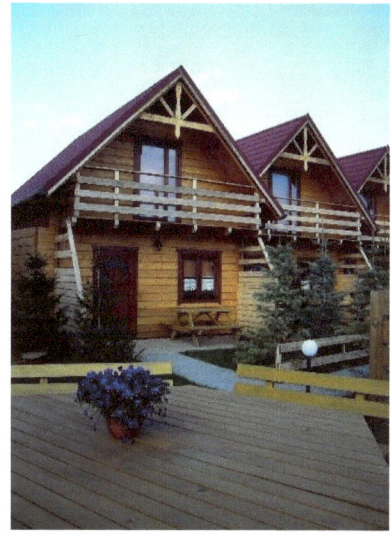
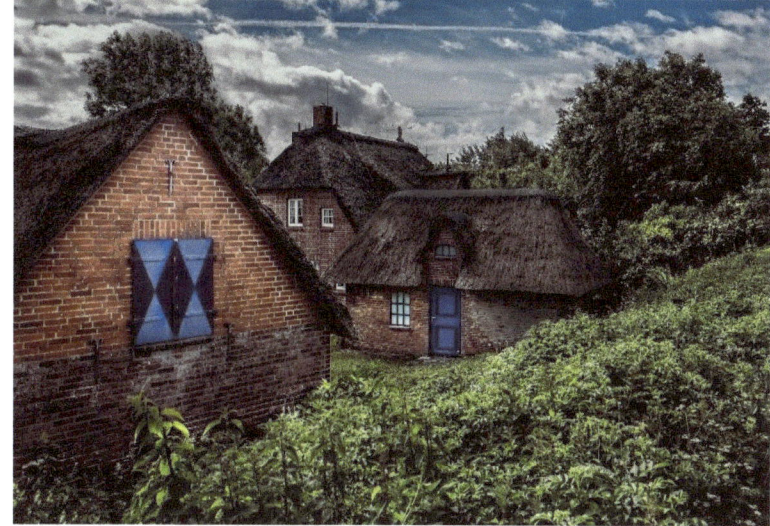

Thatch and Reeds

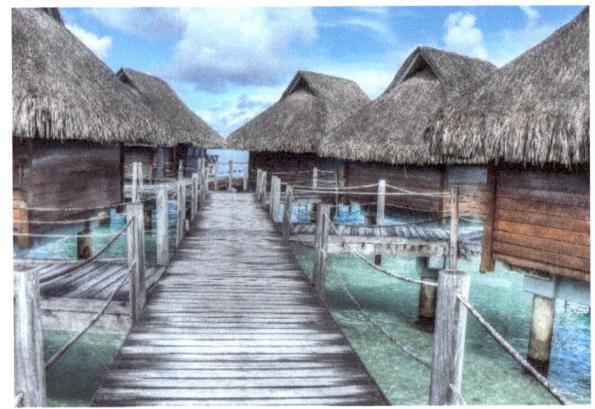
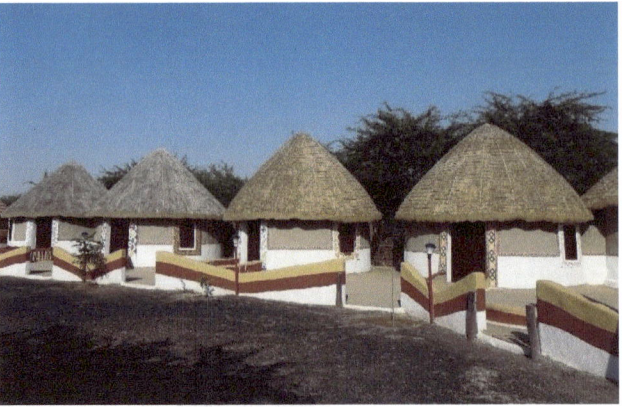
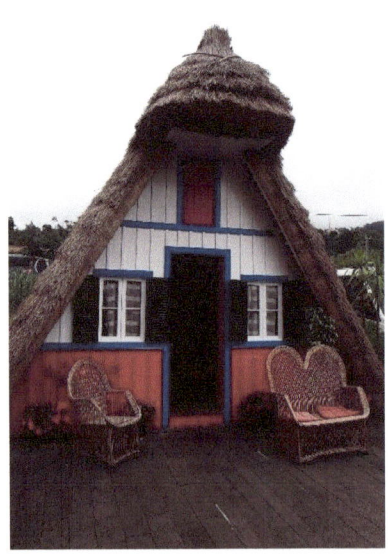

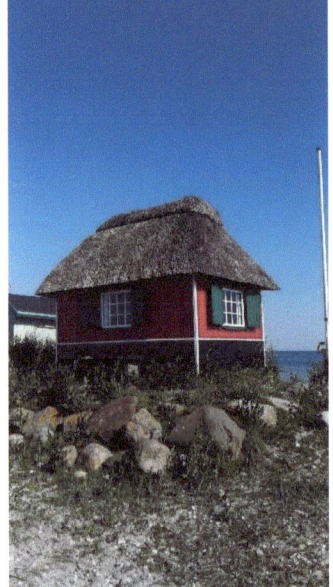
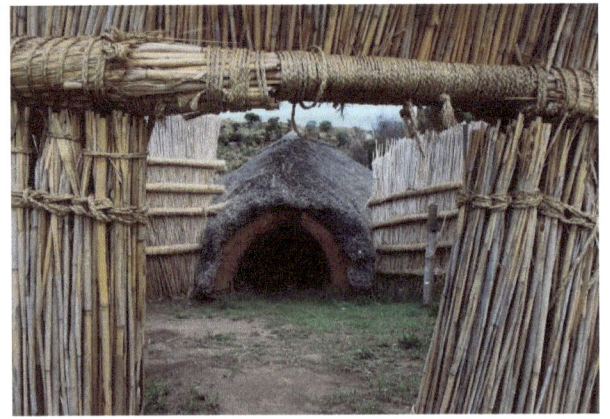
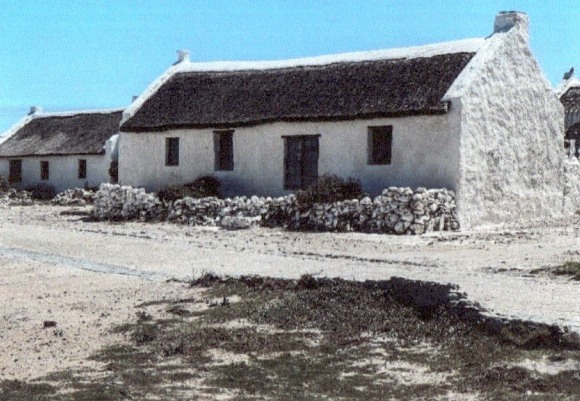

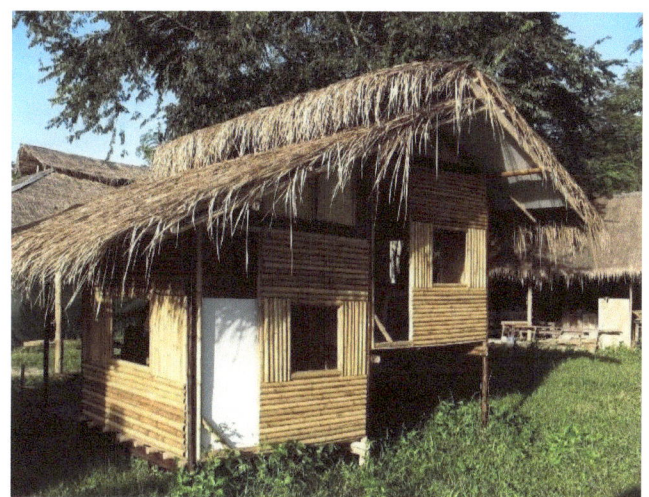
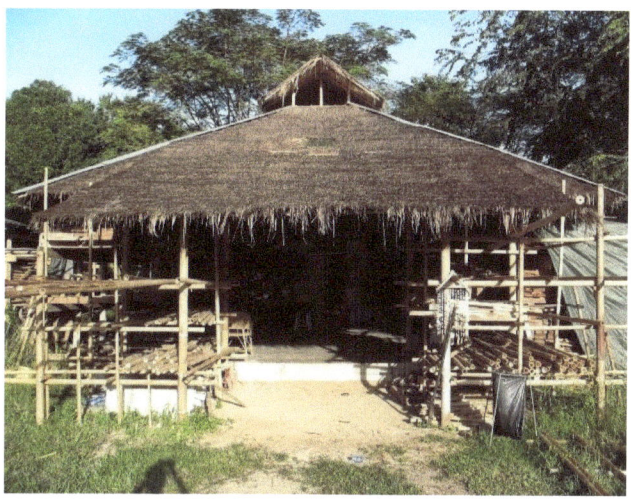
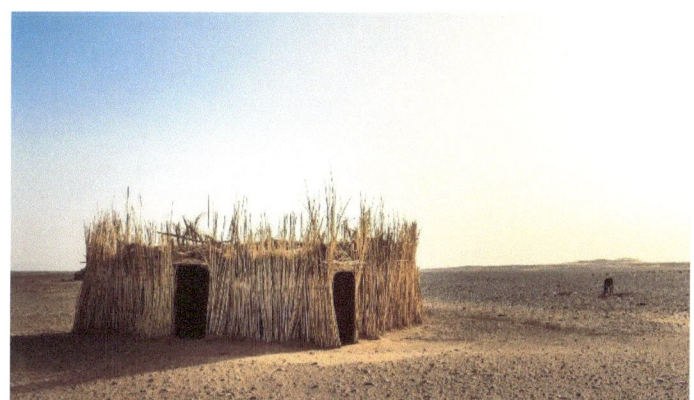
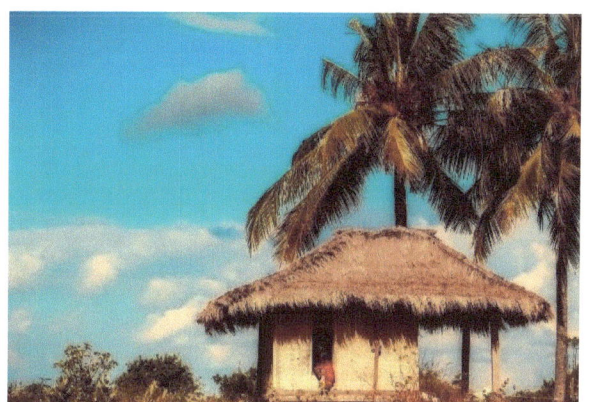

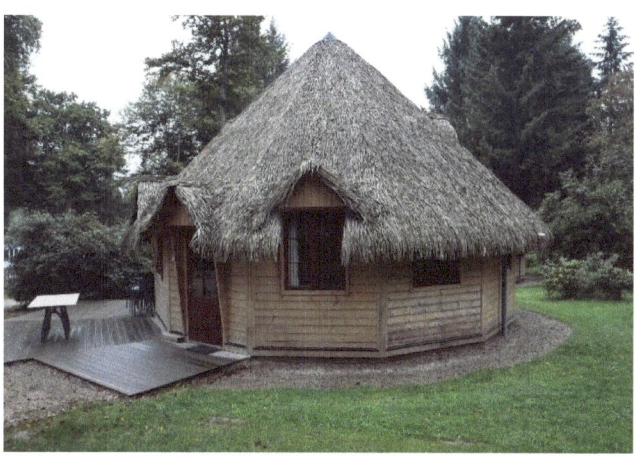
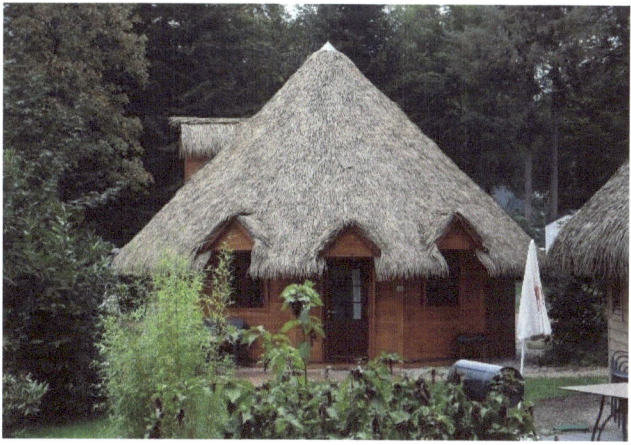

Yurts

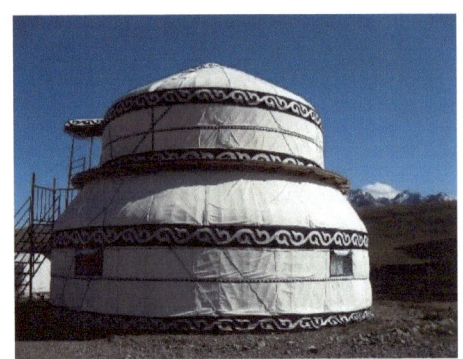
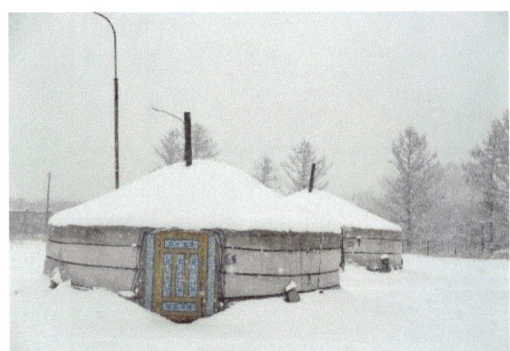
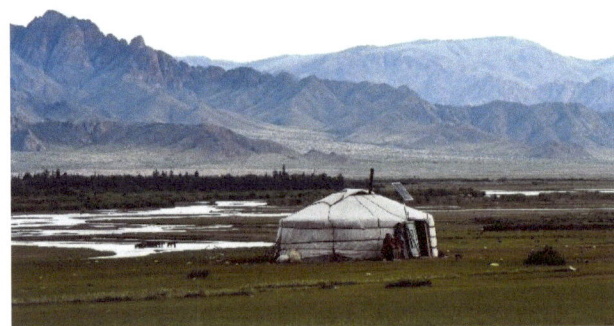
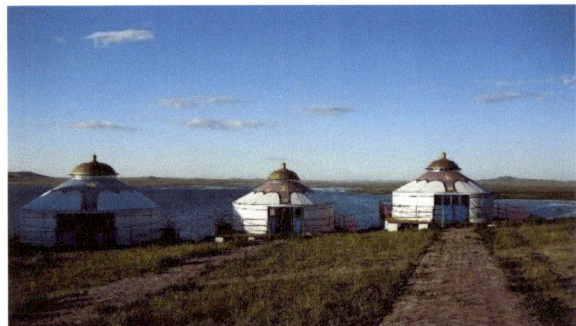
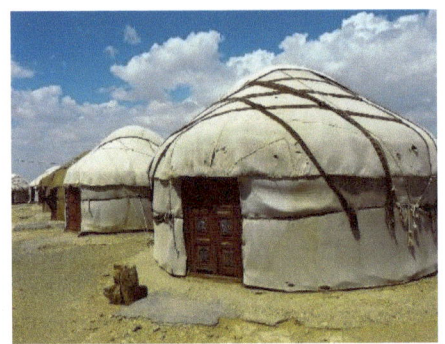
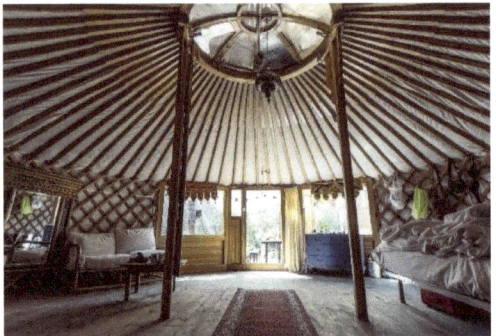
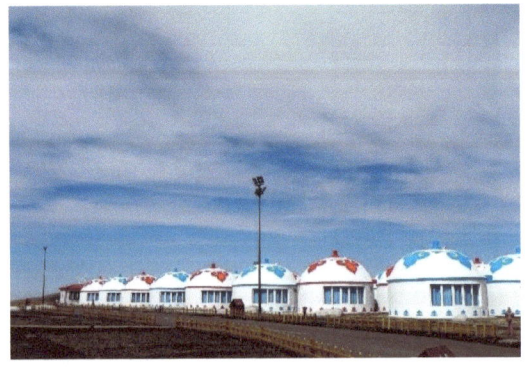
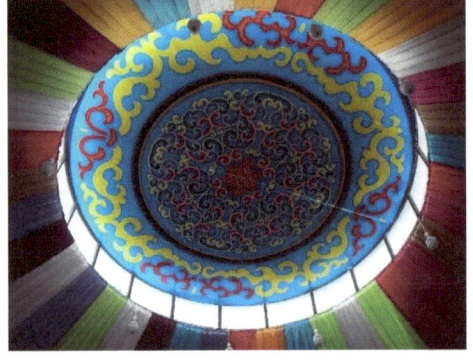

Tipis & Wigwam

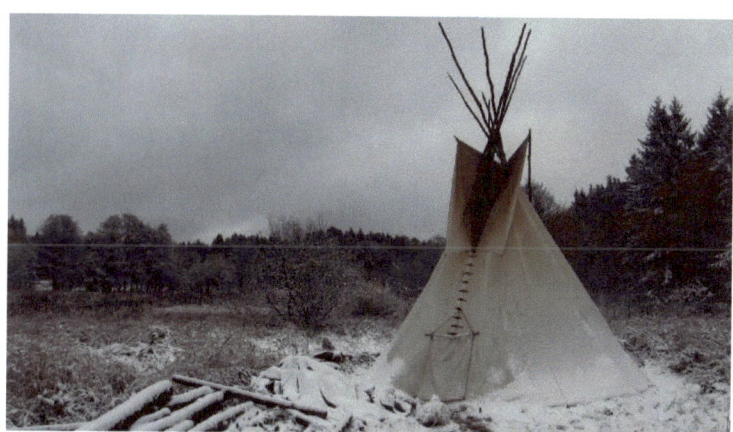 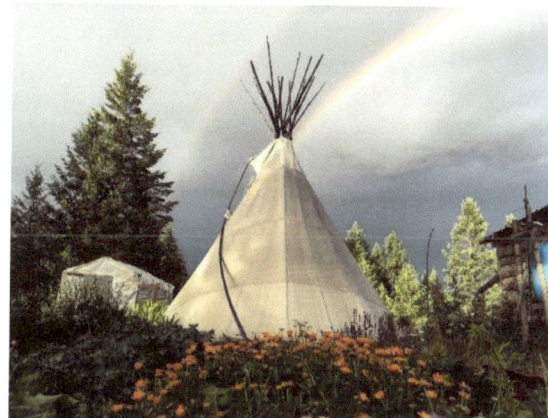

Tipi built by Native Peoples in North America

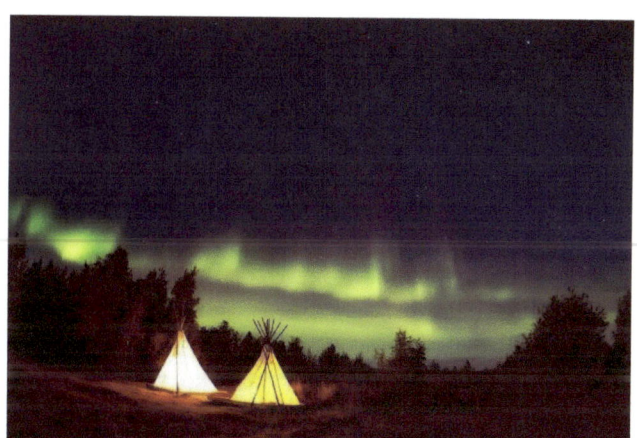 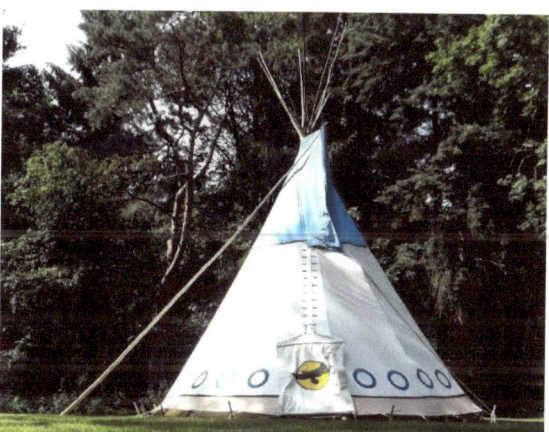

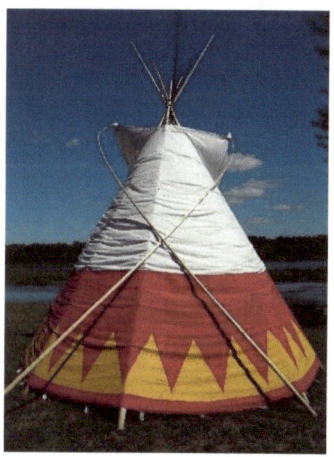 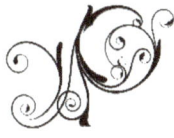 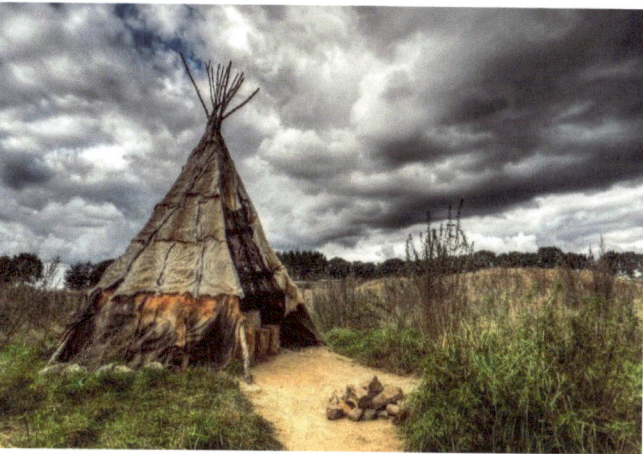

Wigwam home of the Northeastern Tribes

Whimsical

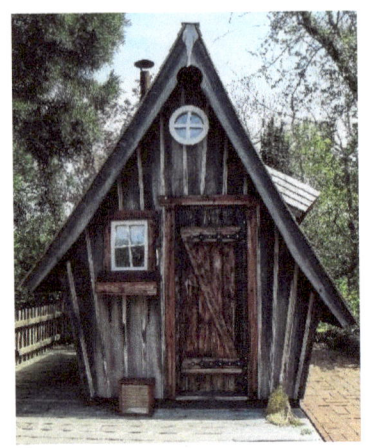
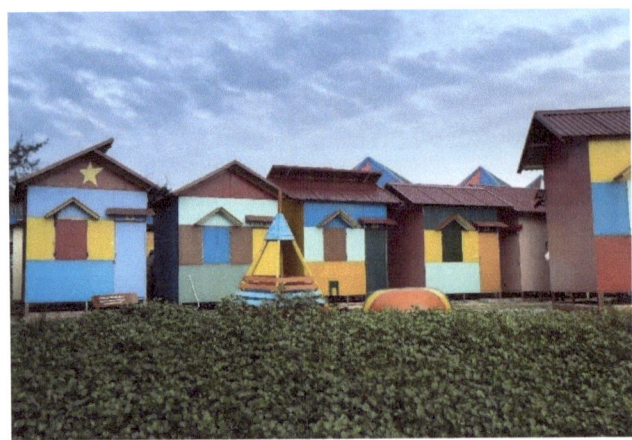
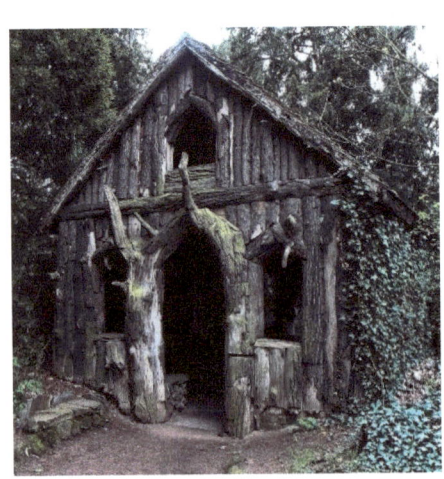
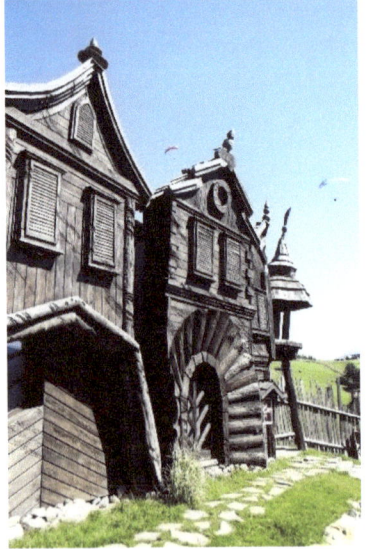
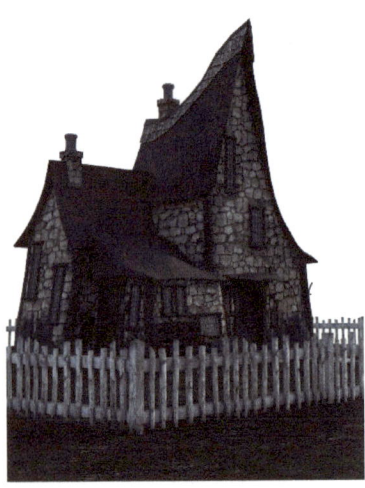
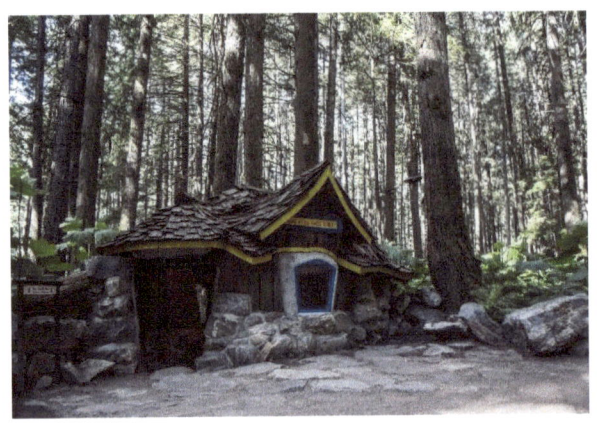
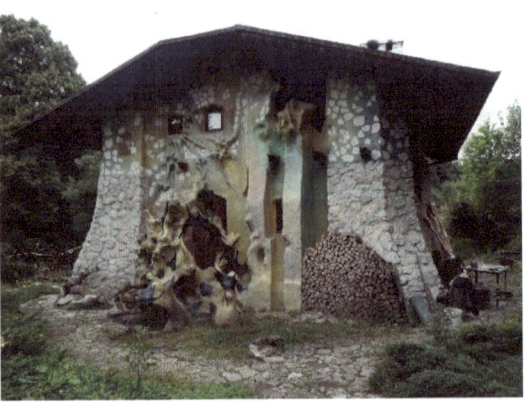

Other Stuff

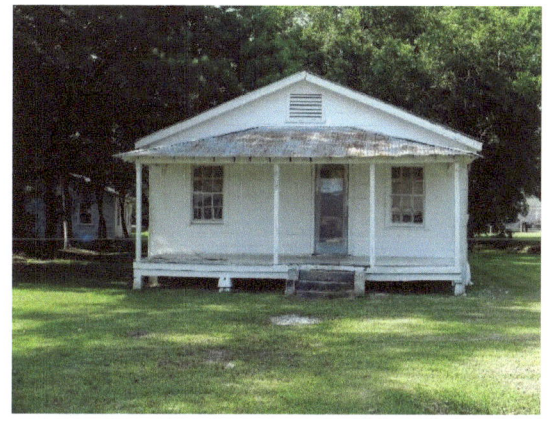
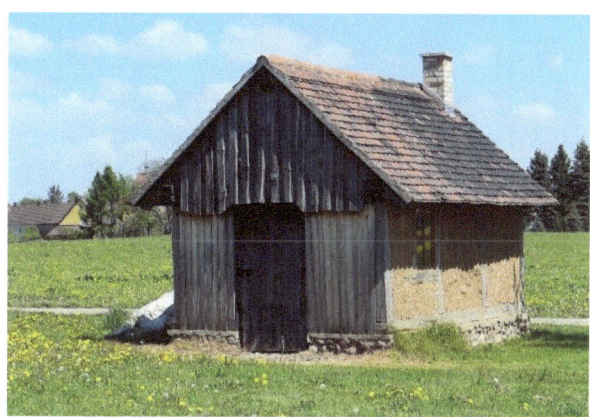
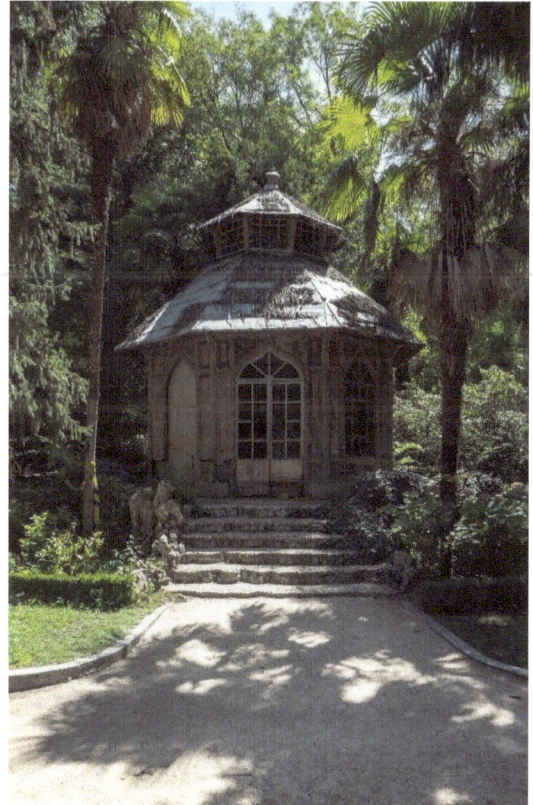
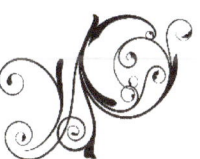
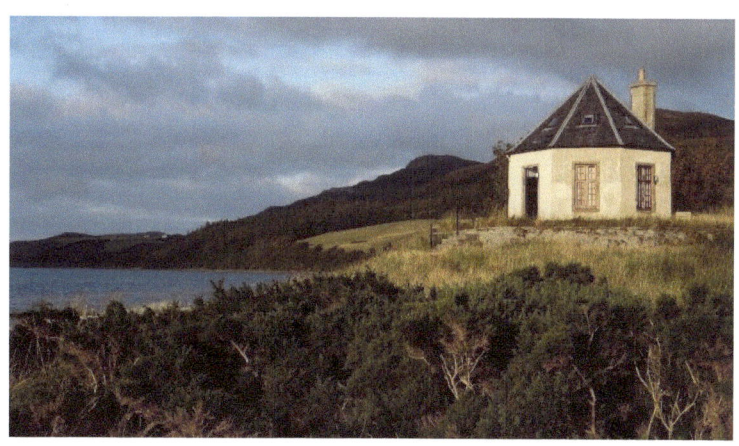

Wheels

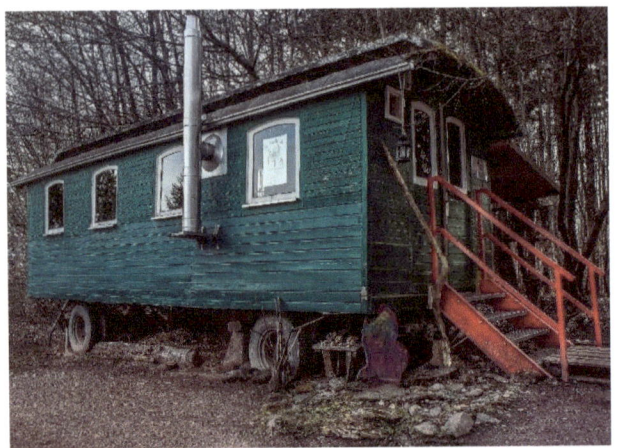
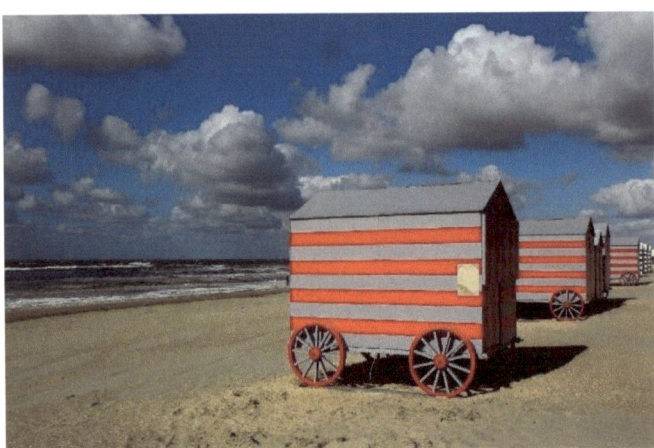
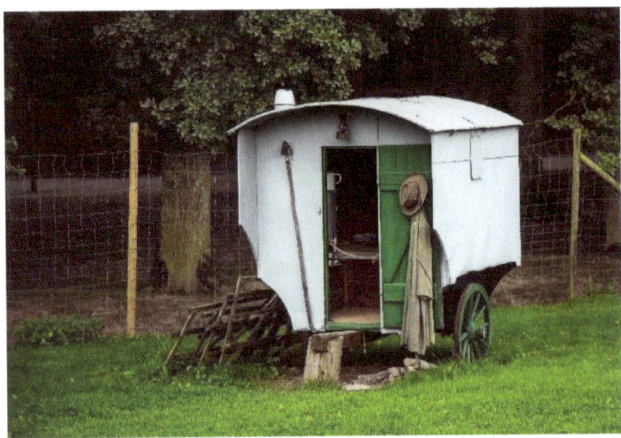
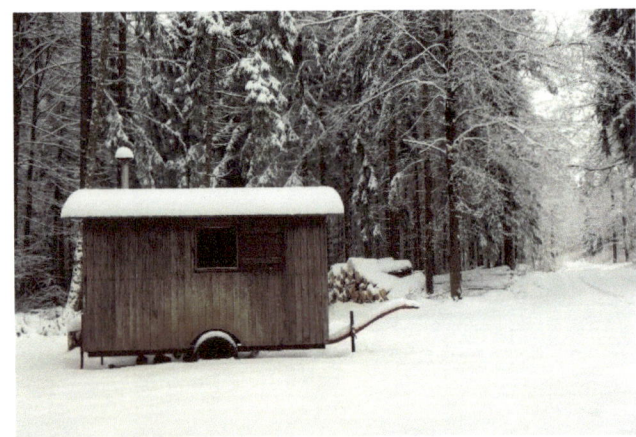
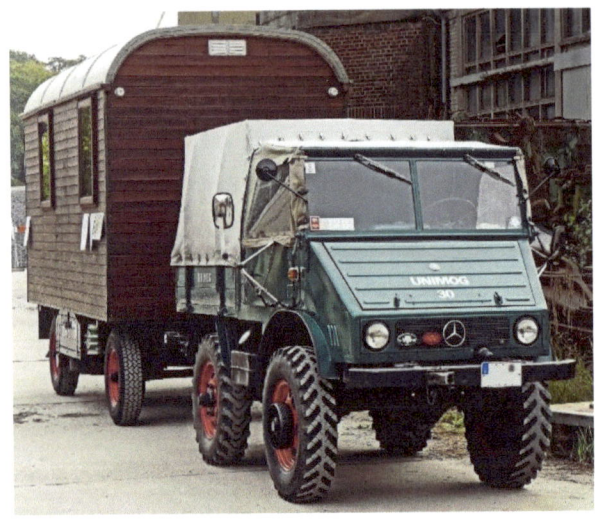
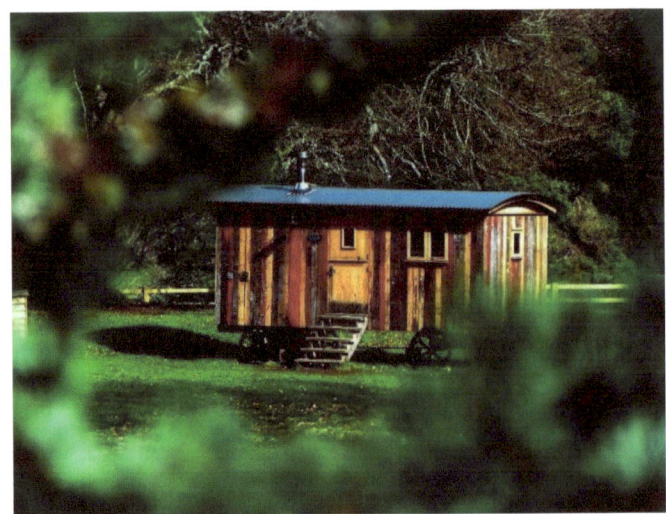

Privies

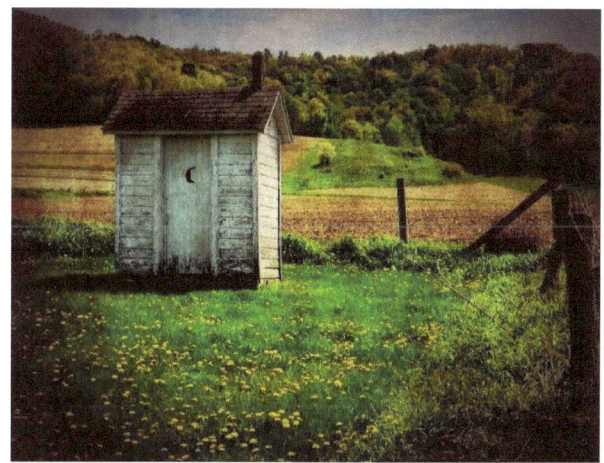
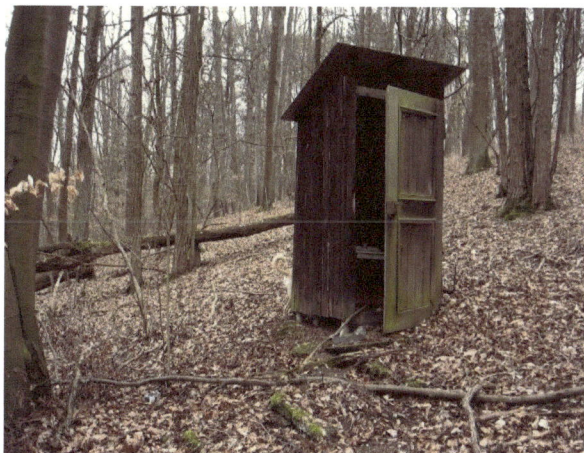
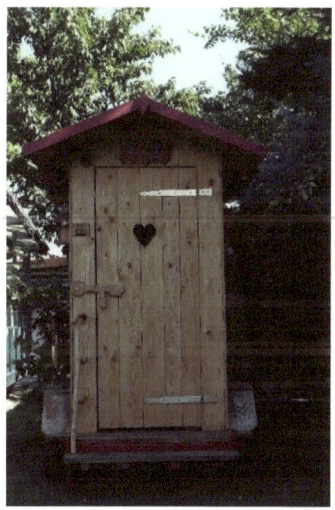
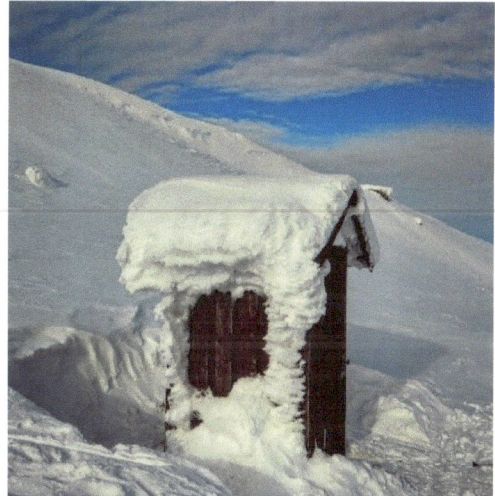
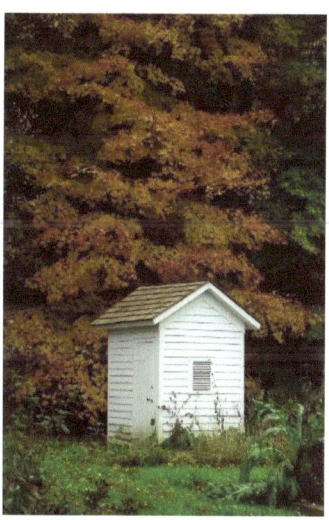
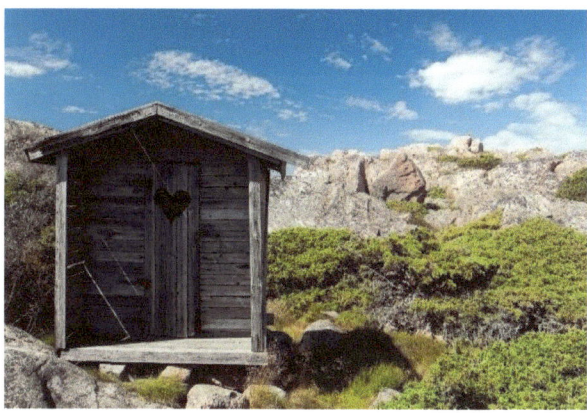
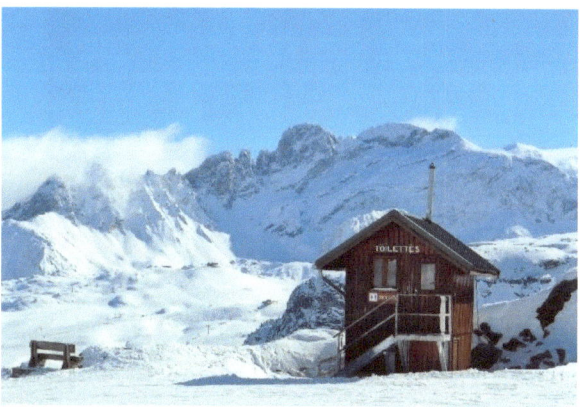

Domes

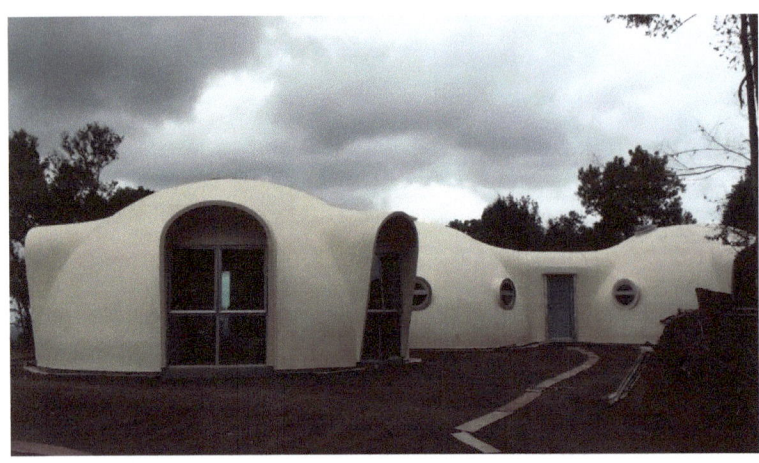
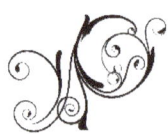
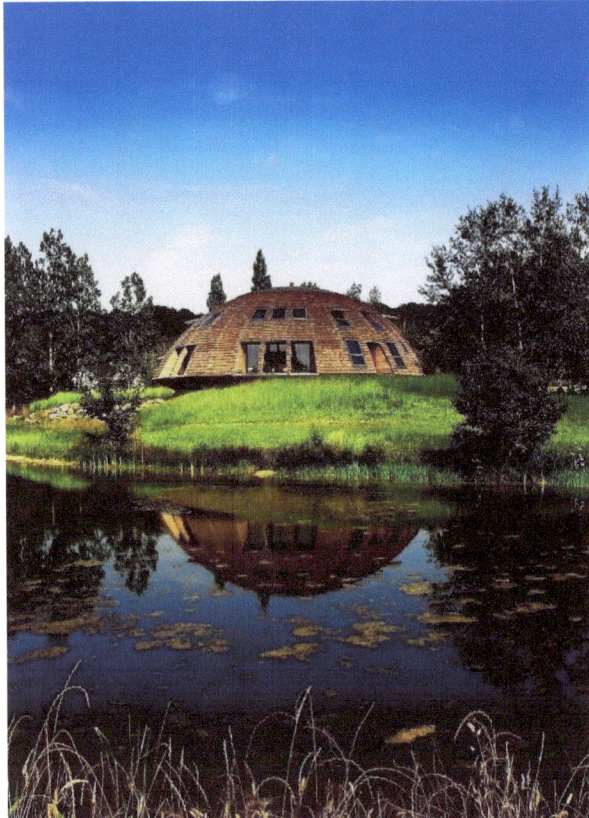
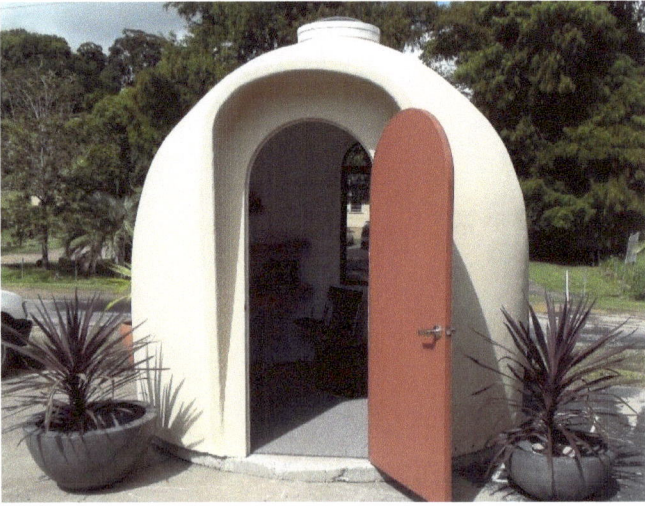
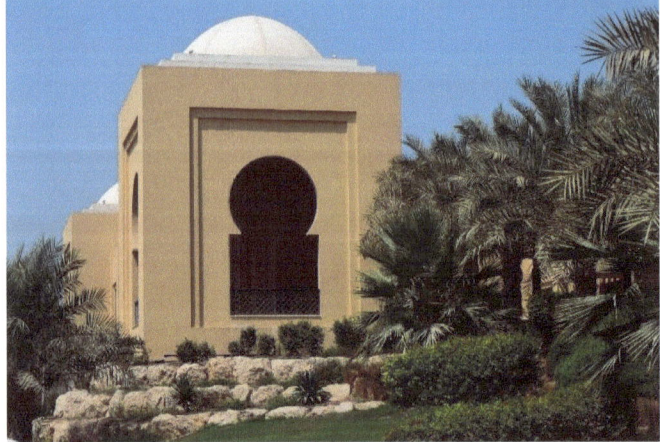

Sheds

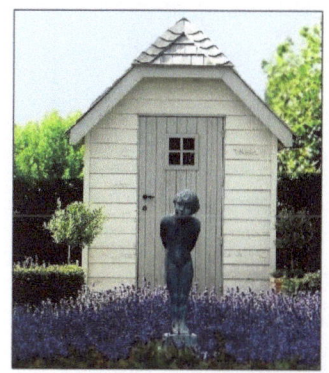
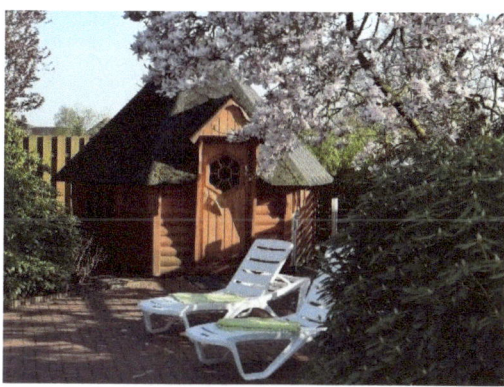
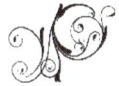
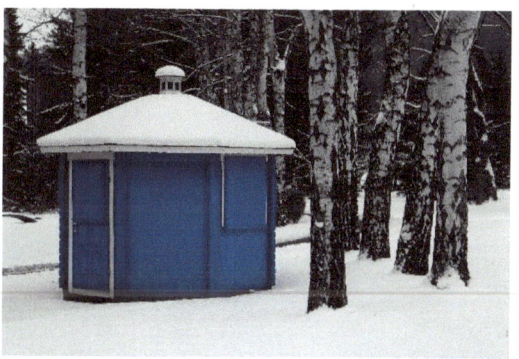
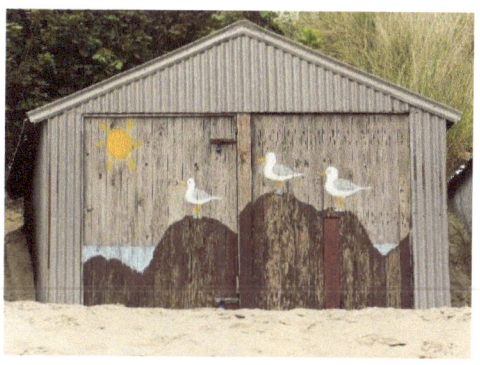
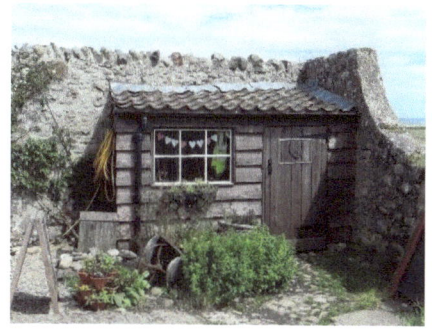
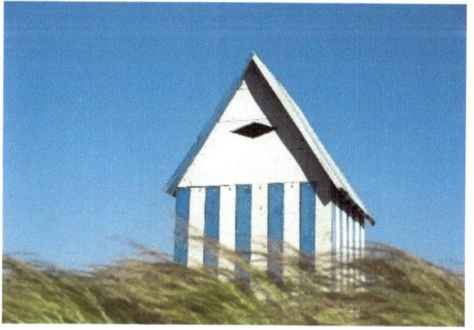

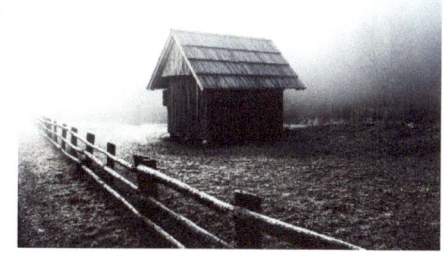
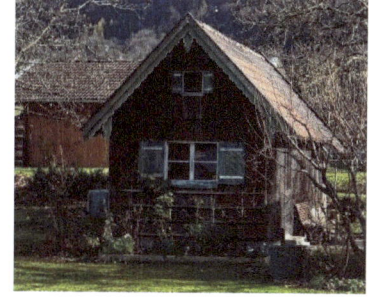

Treehouses

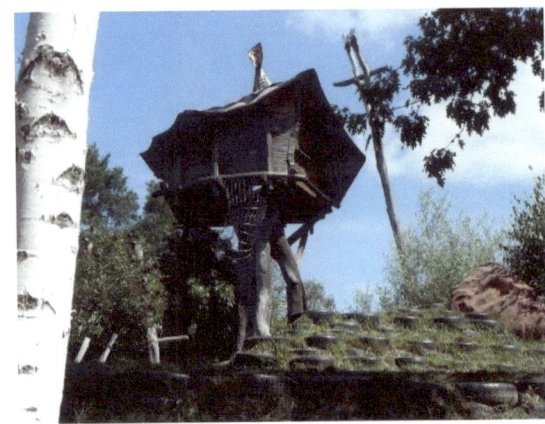
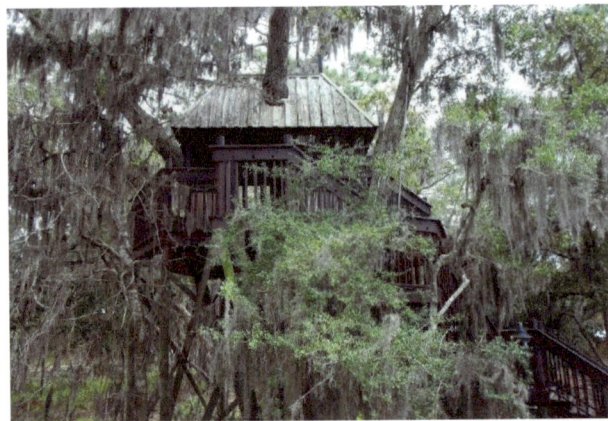
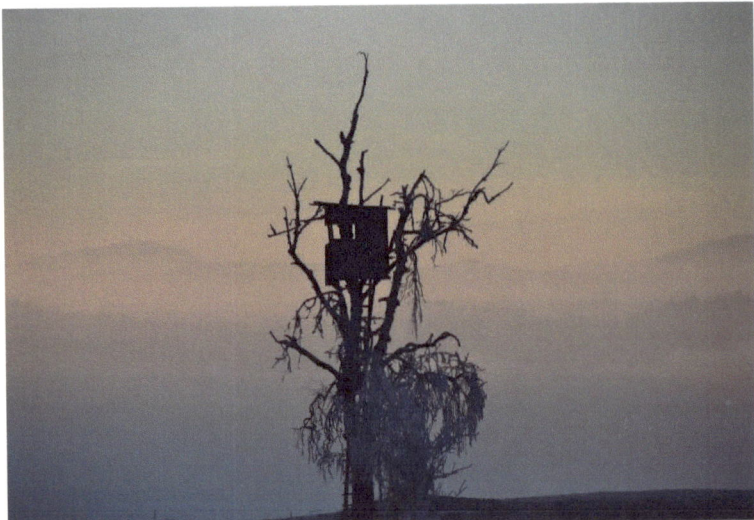
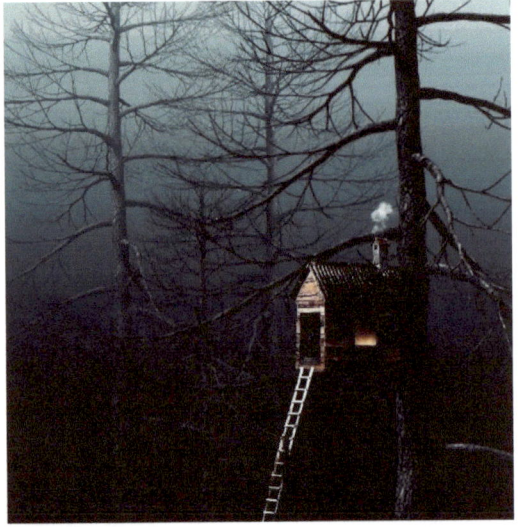
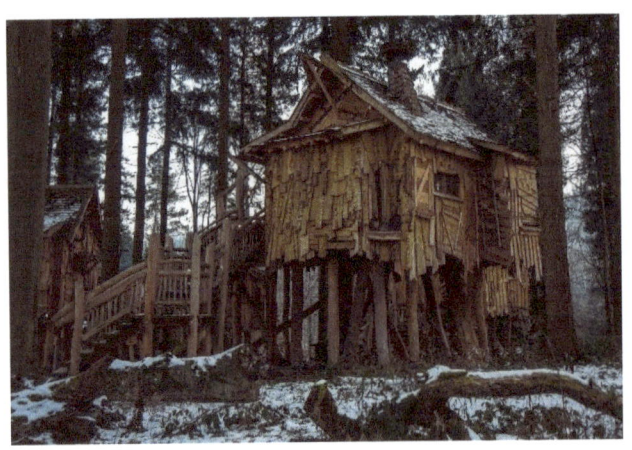
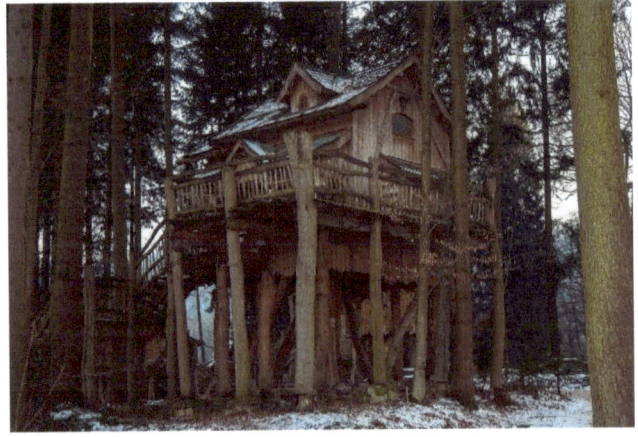

ABOUT THE AUTHOR

Sharon Buydens has written books on tiny houses, passive solar homes,
green (eco-friendly) building and alternative construction, among other topics.
This book is the first color version in a series of picture books / photobooks that she plans to publish.